The DAY The SKY
SPLIT
APART

INVESTIGATING a COSMIC MYSTERY

ROY A. GALLANT

Atheneum Books for Young Readers

For Katya

ATHENEUM BOOKS FOR YOUNG READERS
An imprint of Simon & Schuster Children's Publishing Division
Simon & Schuster
1230 Avenue of the Americas
New York, NY 10020

Book design by Virginia Pope
The text for this book is set in 11-point Berling Roman.
Manufactured in the United States of America
First edition
10   9   8   7   6   5   4   3   2   1

Library of Congress Cataloging-in-Publication Data

Gallant, Roy A.
    The day the sky split apart : investigating a cosmic mystery / Roy A.
Gallant.— 1st ed.
        p.   cm.
    Includes bibliographic references.
    ISBN 0-689-80323-0
    1. Tunguska meteorite—Juvenile literature. 2. Meteorites—Research—
Russia (Federation)—Siberia—Juvenile literature. 3. Scientific expeditions
—Russia (Federation)—Siberia—Juvenile literature. [1. Tunguska meteorite. 2.
Meteorites. 3. Scientific expeditions—Russia (Federation)—Siberia.]—I. Title.
QB756.T8G35 1995   94-48002
523.5'1'095753—dc20   CIP
                                                           AC

The Tunguska meteorite problem is an unsolved scientific problem wrapped in legends and pseudoscientific speculations, an arena of a struggle between scientific and "near" scientific ideas and opinions.

—Valentin Tsvetkov

On March 23, 1989 an object about 300 meters in diameter passed by Earth traveling at nearly 65,000 kilometers per hour. It missed Earth by about 640,000 kilometers, just 1.5 times the distance to the Moon. Had it struck Earth, it would have impacted with an energy equivalent of over 2,000 one-megaton hydrogen bombs. The most astonishing aspect of this event is that the object was not discovered until after it had passed Earth!

—NASA
"Near-Earth-Object Interception Workshop"

ACKNOWLEDGMENTS

Several people played key roles in making this book possible, most of them Russians. The prime mover is Ekaterina (Kathy) Rossovskaya, colleague and friend from Siberia who proposed the idea for this book early in 1992. She made all the arrangements for the Russian Academy of Sciences to invite me to join its 1992 International Tunguska Expedition. Then there were arrangements for travel across Russia, lodging, two and a half months of interviews with scientists, journalists, physicians, politicians, academicians, searches for recent and decades-old documents about the Tunguska explosion—including papers by L. A. Kulik and I. M. Suslov, and many others—and nonstop spontaneous interpreting. And finally, once home, there were months of work translating the dozens of taped interviews and the two-foot-high stack of documents in Russian. My deepest thanks to you, Kathy.

I wish also to thank Academician Nickolai V. Vasiliev, who has coordinated the scientific research of the twenty-nine annual Tunguska investigations since 1963. Beginning with our first meeting in Siberia, he devoted many hours recounting details of the history of the Tunguska investigations over the past several decades. He also expressed his views of the numerous hypotheses that have been put forward over the years in an attempt to explain what it was that exploded on that June morning in 1908 in what has come to be called "the cosmic mystery of the century." I also wish to thank Nickolai for reading relevant sections of my manuscript for accuracy.

My thanks also to Gennadi Andreev, director of the Astronomical Observatory of Tomsk State University (Siberia) and codirector (with Academician Vasiliev) of the ongoing Tunguska expeditions, for issuing the formal invitation that made it possible for me to visit Russia and take part in the 1992 international expedition.

These acknowledgments would be glaringly incomplete without including special thanks to two remarkable men. One is Yuriy Kandyba who, like Kathy, has trod hundreds of kilometers of the "enchanted" taiga during several Tunguska expeditions over the years. Kandyba's knowledge of that wilderness area is remarkable, and it served us well as he led Kathy and me to regions of the Tunguska epicenter rarely visited. I owe Kandyba thanks also for relating many details of the early history of the Tunguska expeditions, for allowing me to copy a number of archival photographs, and for permitting me to use his map showing the location of various eyewitness accounts of the 1908 blast. Access to other accounts of the blast involved many hours of searches through old Krasnoyarsk newspapers, and other Russian publications, by Kathy's mother, Dr. Tatyana Lvovna Rossovskaya.

The other remarkable person is Vitaliy Voronov, whose skills as a hunter and whose knowledge of the Evenki (Tungus people) is extensive and whose reputation as a hunter extends to many and distant parts of Siberia. I also am indebted to Irena, Vitaliy's charming wife, whose drawings and paintings so ably capture the aura of the Evenki people.

In Moscow, in Krasnoyarsk, and during the expedition

itself, I was privileged to spend time with a number of scientific investigators, some seasoned and some new to the area. Chief among them is Yevgeniy Kolesnikov, the well-known cosmic isotopic chemist of Moscow University and head of its potassium-argon radiometric dating laboratory. Kolesnikov has been involved in the Tunguska investigations for more than fifteen years and is the leading proponent of the Tunguska event having been a comet. I thank Yevgeniy for reading sections of my manuscript for accuracy. Another chief investigator is Alyona Boyarkina, veteran expedition member for thirty-four years and author of some one hundred academic papers on the Tunguska event. For many of those years she searched hundreds of square kilometers for meteoric matter imbedded in peat; more recently she has been studying geomagnetic anomalies of the soils of the area near and at the epicenter of the explosion. My thanks also to Karin Junghans, a specialist in remote sensing from Munchen, Germany, for providing a copy of her report, "The Analyses of Remote Sensing of the Tunguska Event." My deserved thanks are due to Valentin Tsvetkov, scientific director of the Moscow Planetarium and recognized authority in meteoric science, for sharing with me his work on the 1947 Sikhote-Alin meteorite explosion over eastern Siberia, and for his views of how an analysis of that event might help build a behavioral model of the dispersal of microscopic matter during the Tunguska explosion.

And finally, my thanks to Farley Mowat for permission to reprint a short passage from his book *The Siberians*, published by Little, Brown and Company, © by Farley Mowat, 1970.

My trip to the Tunguska region of Siberia, and participation in the 1992 expedition, were sponsored by my home institution, the Southworth Planetarium, the University of Southern Maine.

CONTENTS

	Preface	xiii
One	*"Surely the God Ogdy Has Landed Here!"*	1
	A Fireball Brighter than the Sun	1
	A Fire God and Light Nights	4
	Scientific Sleuths Take Notice	6
Two	*Eyewitness Accounts*	8
	Reports from Within the Area of Felled Trees	11
	Reports from Outside the Area of Felled Trees	13
	Kulik Interviews Eyewitnesses	15
Three	*The "Sleeping Land"*	18
	A Land of Eternal Frost	19
	Cloud Merchants and Wet Fences	22
	The Siberian Taiga	25
Four	*The First "Expedition" to the Epicenter's Edge*	27
	Susdalev's Plan	29
	Kulik Finds a Friend	30
	Where Meteorites Come From	32

Five	*Kulik's Search Begins*	36
	Other Accounts of a 1908 Blast	37
	A Meteorite Treasure?	41
	Disappointment and Hope	44
Six	*The First Expedition, and a Shaman's Tale*	46
	A Flight Path for the Cosmic Visitor	47
	Kulik Gets His Expedition	48
	A Reluctant Lyuchetkan Is Won Over	51
	Lyuchetkan Says "No"	58
	Who Are the Tungus?	61
	The Shaman's Tale	65
Seven	*Kulik Finds the Epicenter*	67
	In Kulik's Wake	68
	The Churgim Creek and Mount Cascade	72
	Burn Scars and the "Telegraph-Pole Forest"	76
	A Diet of *Puchki* and, Maybe, the Horse?	79
Eight	*The Expeditions of 1928 and 1929–1930*	82
	The 1928 Expedition	83
	Kulik Loses His Crew	86
	Negative Results and the Return Home	87
	The Third Expedition—1929–1930	89
	Digging Into the Suslov Crater	89
	Kulik's Last Expeditions	97
Nine	*What Was It?*	100
	Explorers from Mars?	101
	Expeditions Resumed—and Three Surprises	103
	Meteoroids and Microspherules	106
	Could It Have Been a Comet?	107
	Other Lines of Research	115
	Could It Have Been an Asteroid?	116
	Could It Have Been Antimatter?	118
	Could It Have Been a Black Hole?	120
	Where Matters Stand Now	123

Ten	*Target Earth!*	124
	Hits and Misses	125
	Case of the Missing Planet	129
	How Were the Asteroids Formed?	131
	Earth's Greatest "Murder" Mystery	134
	Was the Cosmic-Culprit Idea Testable?	136
	When the Chicxulub Asteroid Struck	138
Eleven	*Need for an Early Warning System*	142
	First Detection, Then Evasion or Destruction	143
	Nuclear Warheads for the Cosmos	145
	"Brilliant Mountains"	146
	Further Reading	148
	Index	153

PREFACE

BY ACADEMICIAN NICKOLAI VASILIEV,

Member of the Committee for Meteorites,
Russian Academy of Sciences

*T*he destiny of a scientist is inseparable from the problem that that scientist is investigating. Perhaps there is no better example of this in the history of science than the way the destiny of the father of Russian meteoric science, Leonid Alexeivich Kulik, was shaped by his obsession to unravel the mystery of the Tunguska "meteorite." It has never been proved that the 1908 event was a meteorite, although to the end Kulik believed that his tireless search would one day uncover a telltale nugget of cosmic iron. Even though Kulik failed to find his meteorite, the search did not end with his death during World War II. Continuing attempts to learn the nature of that devastating explosion have become one of the most thrilling scientific puzzles of our century.

When we examine the Tunguska event we must underline its many implications. Solving the mystery cannot be regarded narrowly as a problem of Russian science only. It touches everyone who lives on this fragile planet. As we study our planet and peer into space with the marvelous new instruments of physics and astronomy, we increase our understanding of the significant role that the cosmos has played, and continues to play, in shaping the destiny of our planet as a habitable world, and of directing the course of all its life through time. For instance, there can be no doubt that Earth has undergone intensive cosmic bombardment by asteroids and comets many times in its history. These cannonades have led to the extinction of many biological species, have changed the positions of the magnetic poles, and have caused many other events that have been significant in the continuing development of the organic world.

The Tunguska explosion over the Siberian wilderness was one such cosmic event, and the most awesome that has taken place in recorded history. The equivalent of about 40 megatons of TNT (some 10^{24} ergs), it exceeded by approximately 2,000 times the force of the Hiroshima atomic bomb explosion of 1945. Had the Tunguska explosion happened some two hours later, it would have occurred over Saint Petersburg, and the number of victims would have been in the tens or hundreds of thousands.

Not only do we not know what that cosmic body was, but we do not know when another like it, or one even more destructive, will collide with Earth. There is no doubt that there will be others. The big question is not "if," but "when?" On March 23, 1989 an asteroid with a diameter about 300 meters—three times the length of a football playing field—and traveling at nearly 65,000 kilometers an hour missed colliding with Earth by only 640,000 kilometers, just 1.5 times the Moon's distance from us. And no one saw it approach. Also in the late 1980s a large meteorite blasted a crater 15 meters in diameter only 3 kilometers from the border of the city of Sterlytomack in the European part of Russia. The explosion would have caused death and much destruction had it made a direct hit within the city. Consequently, we must continue to regard the cosmos as a source of potential danger that could lead to a catastrophe of huge scale.

Since Kulik's first expedition to Tunguska, investigators have amassed volumes of data that have given us insights into the event—ranging from numerous eyewitness accounts on that fateful morning to magnetic surveys and analyses of soil and biological samples of vegetation collected over hundreds of square kilometers of the epicenter region. A thorough study of those data has revealed a number of facts about the uniqueness of the Tunguska object.

First, we may conclude that the object never struck the ground. The fanlike pattern of trees felled by the blast—still very much visible today—suggests that the explosion occurred about 6 kilometers above the forest. In addition to felling trees over an area of some 2,200 square kilometers, the fiery blast enflamed an area of some 1,000 square kilometers within the blowdown region. What happened to the object? There are grounds to suspect that whatever remained of the object after the blast skipped back out of the atmosphere and continued its northwestward journey back into space, much like a flat pebble striking the water surface and skipping back into the air again.

Second, despite decades of drilling, digging, and otherwise combing the epicenter region, not a single solid piece of the object has been identified. Yet its mass should have been not less than 100,000 tons. Because only the usual amount of meteoric dust that rains down on Earth virtually everywhere has been found in the epicenter region, is it possible that the Tunguska object was significantly different from ordinary iron and stone meteorites? To date, we cannot answer.

Third, the bright flash of the mystery object's explosion over the Podkamennaya [Stony] Tunguska River was only one spectacular episode in a complex chain of unusual events occurring in a much greater region surrounding north-central Siberia during the summer of 1908. There were what have come to be called "white nights," associated with colossal optical fireworks that covered the huge territory of western Siberia,

Middle Asia, the European parts of Russia, and parts of Europe. During these white nights it was so light that one could read the face of a watch and the small print of a newspaper. By day, the Sun was often ringed by beautiful haloes.

There also were bright displays of noctilucent, or "night-shining," clouds high in the atmosphere. The base surfaces of these clouds have been estimated to cover some 14 million square kilometers. And there were unusual and beautiful multicolored twilights caused by changes in the refractive property of the atmosphere at a height of from 40 to 70 kilometers. The fall of metal or stone meteorites is not announced by such spectacular displays. All these light displays had begun around June 22, before the explosion, but reached a colossal maximum on the night of June 30, the date of the explosion. After June 30 the frequency and intensity of all these effects died away relatively rapidly. Following the explosion, scientists working in the observatory on Mt. Wilson, California, reported a marked decrease in the transparency of the atmosphere.

Fourth, after the Tunguska object exploded, magnetic storms were recorded over a period of some hours by the Irkutsk observatory several hundred kilometers from the epicenter. The storms' graph profiles resemble those produced by atmospheric nuclear test explosions. So far, no one has put forward a satisfactory explanation for the profile pattern. Geophysical observatories in many locations in the Eastern and Western hemispheres registered the blast's shock wave. The seismic waves were recorded in Irkutsk, Tashkent, Tbilisi, and Jena (Germany).

The fifth peculiarity is the series of biological consequences following the explosion. Within the epicenter region, and along the presumed trajectory of the object, there was an increased growth rate of vegetation. There also has been an increased rate in the frequencies of certain plant mutations.

This list could be continued. And the more we discover

about the many different effects presumed to have been caused by the Tunguska event, the harder pressed we are to explain the nature of the object. There are so many unanswered and mysterious components of the Tunguska catastrophe that we still are not at the point in our scientific sleuthing when we categorically can rule out the object being a comet or an asteroid, for example.

To date, our scientific community has managed to save 4,000 square kilometers of the Tunguska region as a national preserve for the next twenty years. But we think this is not enough time to do the ecological monitoring that should be done. Our initiative now is to extend protection of the preserve under the supervision of UNESCO. Its preservation is of concern not only to Russia, but to people of all nations. Those who have been privileged to work at the Tunguska site and have seen the land being churned by the tractor treads of state oil exploration crews sense the urgency of preserving the region. To us it is evident that our work should be continued before time and machines destroy all remaining traces of the "cosmic mystery of the century."

This book relates Roy Gallant's firsthand experiences at the explosion site during our 1992 expedition, an overview of the first expeditions to the site in the 1920s and 1930s, recent and ongoing scientific attempts to untangle the riddle, and finally confronts the inevitable question, "What are the chances of its happening again?"

Following page: Siberia is a vast, sprawling land in northern Asia. It extends from the Ural Mountains in the west to the Pacific Ocean in the east; and from Mongolia in the south to the Arctic in the north. Shown on this map is the range of the Tunguska blast as determined by Krinov, deputy director of the 1929-1930 expedition. The solid line shows the southeast to northwest entry path of the cosmic object. 1) shows the blast site; 2) limit of the blast effects that could be seen; 3) distance to which the explosion could be heard; and 4) the expedition's route from Tayshet to the blast site.   MAP BY RICK BRITTON

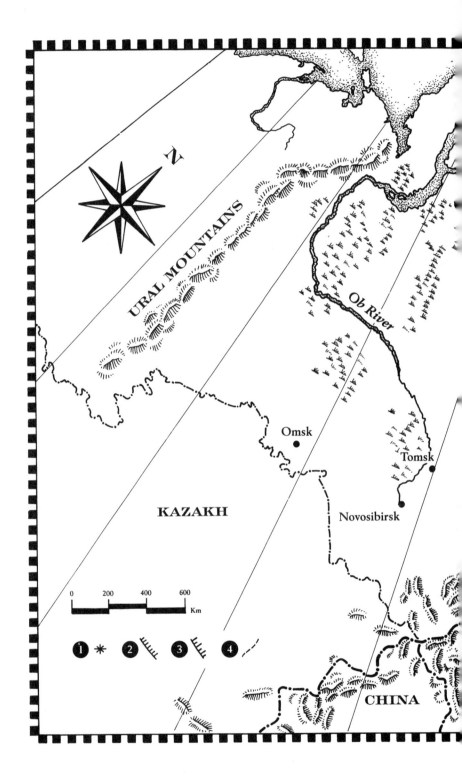

URAL MOUNTAINS

N

Ob River

Omsk

Tomsk

Novosibirsk

KAZAKH

0   200   400   600
                    Km

1 ✳   2 ⌁   3 ⌁   4 ⌁

CHINA

KARA SEA

LAPTEV SEA

Yenisei River

SIBERIA

Lena River

Stony Tunguska River
(Podkamennaya)

Strelka

Kashmo River

Vanavara

Yeniseysk

Kezhma

Lena River

Angara River

Bodaybo

Krasnoyarsk

Ilimsk

Kirensk

Kansk

Yenisei River

Tayshet

Minusinsk

Lake Baikal

Irkutsk

MONGOLIA

CHAPTER ONE

"SURELY, *the* GOD OGDY HAS LANDED HERE!"

The explosions were heard in the early morning hours of June 30, 1908, about the time most farmers were already at work in their fields. It was a drama that has occurred countless times in Earth's geological history, and one that surely will play again.

A FIREBALL BRIGHTER THAN THE SUN

Those Tungus tribesmen and Russian fur traders who happen to glance into the Siberian sky that fateful morning are puzzled on seeing a distant bright spot, a "second Sun," approach out of the cloudless southeastern sky, that rapidly grows larger. Their puzzlement then turns to horror as the spot billows into a fireball brighter than the Sun and appears to streak down through the atmosphere directly toward their trading post of Vanavara on the Stony Tunguska River. Behind the monstrous thing is a blazing trail of light some 800 kilometers long—the distance from central Maine to New York City.

The thing, whatever it is, approaches from an azimuth of

Reindeer, tepees, and stores were hurled into the air by the explosion. This is one of the more than 100 paintings based on eyewitness accounts of the Tunguska explosion, by the famous Russian artist Nickolai Federov. In 1939 Kulik invited Federov to the epicenter to interview the local Tungus people and begin his series of paintings. Federov died in 1989.

COURTESY: NATALIA FEDEROVA

115 degrees and rapidly descends at an angle of 30 to 35 degrees above the horizon. With arms raised to shield their faces from the heat and fierce light, their gaze continues to follow the blinding fireball as it moves along a northwestward trajectory until it seems about to disappear over the horizon.

Then the cosmic visitor explodes at about 7:15 A.M. local time while still in the air an estimated 6 kilometers above the sprawling forest and some 70 kilometers northwest of Vanavara. The point of the explosion, as determined by satellite navigation aid (GPS) during our 1992 expedition, was 60° 55'04" N, 101° 56'55" E. The flash of the explosion was to be reported from as far away as 710 kilometers in the village of Znamenskoye in Irkutsk province.

The sky appears to split apart in a rapid series of bursts lasting about half a second and crossing a distance of 15 to 20 kilometers. The deafening roar terrifies children and adults going about their early morning chores. Later, some said the explosions sounded like a "cannonade" that thundered across the countryside for 1,200 kilometers and resounded for several minutes. Others likened the clamor to "a dozen trains all rattling the rails simultaneously." Those closer to ground zero of the explosion are temporarily deafened by the blast. Those nearer are struck dumb and speechless and fall to the ground in a state of shock.

A series of shock waves pulsing through the bedrock causes tepees and frame buildings to shudder. Sod packing is loosened and jolted from log roofs and rains down on startled occupants. Windows are rattled and glass shattered. Fishermen repairing their boats along the banks of the Stony Tunguska River are tossed into the air and flung into the water. Horses stumble over the trembling ground and lose their footing. Dogs are flipped off balance. The shock waves continue through the bedrock. A thousand kilometers away in the southwest, near Kansk, a speeding Trans-Siberian passenger train begins to rattle, and it shakes dozing passengers fearfully awake. Unbelievably, the engineer watches the tracks ahead shiver as if kept moving by an earthquake that doesn't stop. When the rails end their eerie dance he nervously creeps the train along to the next station where he examines each car and tries to calm the frightened passengers. No, he cannot tell them what happened. He is as mystified as they are.

The blast fells trees outward in a radial pattern over an area of some 2,000 square kilometers, more than half the size of Rhode Island. In the hot central region of the epicenter the forest flashes into a soaring column of flame that is visible several hundred kilometers away. The fires burn for weeks, destroying an area of some 1,000 square kilometers. Ash and powdered tundra fragments sucked skyward to a height of some 20 kilometers by the fiery vortex are caught up in the global air circulation and carried around the world. As the debris mixes with the air over Tunguska, condensation triggers a "black rain" of mud and ash.

A FIRE GOD AND LIGHT NIGHTS

How could the migrant Evenki hunters explain the fireball explosions and the terrifying events that followed the blasts? The Evenki (as the Tungus are called by the Russians) were not an educated people. They practiced shamanism, a religion based on animism. Animism is the belief that objects in nature contain a spirit or life force. The Evenki believed that their spiritual leaders—shamans—were able to communicate with both good and evil spirits, and that they served as mediums between the spirit world and the living world. The shamans' power over their tribes, and their great prestige, also gave them authority to maintain social order. Some of the shamans who ruled over Evenki tribes in the Tunguska region told their people that their disobedience had enraged the god of fire, Ogdy, and that his fiery fist was but a warning should their disobedience continue. So matters rested for many years. The rest of the world remained uninformed of the fireball explosion. Reports of events that occurred in the remote regions of Tunguska only rarely, and then quite by chance, reached the outside world. And news of the fireball explosion was not to get out for many years.

However, the rest of the world knew that *something* had happened deep within central Siberia. After all, major seismograph stations in key locations around the globe had recorded tremors produced by the blast, and workers at those stations interpreted those records as just that—tremors caused by an earthquake somewhere in northern Asia. But there were other telltale signs that something had happened. As noted in the Preface by Academician Vasiliev, they occurred both before and after the presumed earthquake, but no one was to link the events until years later.

The July 3, 1908 issue of the *New York Times* ran a story filed from Berlin about the strange night light displays that were being observed so brightly in the northern sky and discussed all over Europe. They had appeared most intense for the previous two nights—which interestingly happened to be the first two nights after the blast, though no one at the time realized that. The report quoted the director of the Treptow Observatory as saying that "because of the phenomenon's particular brilliancy [the light displays] may be connected with important changes in the Sun's surface, causing electrical discharges."

Reports of bright night displays came from a number of other cities, including Copenhagen, Konigsberg, Madrid, and London. Some said that the sky was so bright that they were able to take photographs at midnight. One report from Holland described the daytime sky on the day of the explosion as heaving in a great wave that crossed the northwestern horizon. So bright and so red was the sky on the evening of the blast that it appeared to be on fire, according to an observer in Antwerp. An observer in England described the eastern sky on July 1 as shining with an "intense green to yellow-gold hue." Twilight on that and the following night, he added, lasted through the night until daybreak. A July 5 article in the *New York Times* filed from London mentioned the midnight sky being so bright toward the north that "police headquarters was rung up by several people who believed that a big fire was raging in the north of London."

The London *Times* reported magnetic disturbances along with the light displays and attributed them to "disturbances in the Sun's prominences." Five hours after the explosion British meteorological stations recorded sudden changes in atmospheric pressure. There were, in fact, two pressure wave surges that twice circled the planet. Letters sent to the *Times* asked if someone could please explain "the cause of so unusual a sight."

SCIENTIFIC SLEUTHS TAKE NOTICE

For reasons as interesting as the cataclysmic event itself, scientific sleuths did not gain entrance to the hostile and remote region of the explosion for nearly twenty years. To this day the remote area is accessible only by helicopter or by foot across 70 kilometers of swamps, bogs, and taiga ruled by the Russian bear. Until 1989 the former Soviet government had kept the region off limits to foreign scientists, unless they were from other communist nations. Today the government's attitude is very different. The welcome mat is out to all foreign scientists. The Russian Academy of Sciences is now eager to attract investigators from the West. Funding to continue the ongoing investigations is needed, as are various high-tech tools and apparatus that the Russians lack.

Despite the decades of ongoing investigations, there is still no consensus about what the visitor from space was, although there are almost as many hypotheses as there have been investigators. And the search is continued each year by astronomers, chemists, geologists, physicists, botanists, biologists, and at least one specialist in remote sensing. There are still others who have never set foot in the region but from thousands of miles away use computer modeling in an attempt to solve the mystery. Whatever it was that came hurtling out of the black of space on that clear June morning of 1908, it delivered the most devastating known assault on the planet in the history of civilization.

CHAPTER TWO

EYEWITNESS
ACCOUNTS

*T*he photograph is a typical one from almost any family album—mother kneeling beside her three-year-old son and her two daughters, aged about six and eight, standing in front of the doorway of their modest home. It is the Tungus family of the absent hunter Ilya Potapovich—who is also known as Lyuchetkan—one of the many eyewitnesses of the Tunguska explosion. He will return to our story later.

Who are these *Tungus* people?

Their racial roots are ancient. They probably originated in the Amur River Basin (see map following preface) in the area where Siberia borders Mongolia and Manchuria. The Tungus call home the sprawling region that extends from the Yenisei River eastward to the Pacific Ocean and north into the tundra and to the edge of the Arctic Ocean. In the 1950s there were about 80,000 remaining Tungus, but their numbers and distinctive culture, at least in the Siberian region, have rapidly declined since then.

Look at the photograph again. The hut of Lyuchetkan is a typical Siberian Tungus tepee made of overlapped layers of the heavy bark of Siberian cedar trees supported from the inside

Lyuchetkan's wife Maria and three children by their tepee. The antennalike object is the skin of a sacrificed young deer displayed to appease the god Havokee and persuade him not to send his iron birds to destroy their home. This photo was taken in October, 1928 by ethnographer Innokenty Suslov.

COURTESY: COMMITTEE ON METEORITES, RUSSIAN ACADEMY OF SCIENCES

and on the outside by up to forty poles, depending on the size of the tepee. In winter the family are warmed by a fire kept burning in a central hearth as the smoke curls out of the chimneylike opening at the tepee's top. Now look at the strange structure supported by a pole at the right of the tepee. It is a reminder of the awful event that shook the planet on the morning of June 30, 1908.

When the object from space came blazing into the sky, exploded, and enflamed more than a thousand square kilometers of forest, it also incinerated an unknown number of tepees and herds of several thousand reindeer. The Tungus tribes kept reindeer as work animals and as providers of milk, meat, and hides. Framed within the structure on the pole in the photograph is the stretched skin of a young deer, sacrificed and displayed as a charm to appease the angry god the Tungus believed had sent the fireball crashing down on them in punishment for their disobedience. The photograph was taken in 1928 by Innokenty Suslov, an ethnographer and one of the first investigators to question eyewitnesses about the event. Although Lyuchetkan's children had not been born at the time of the explosion, he and his wife were then children who witnessed the fearsome event and would remember it always. There were many other eyewitnesses as well, and over the years following 1926 Leonid A. Kulik also collected their accounts. He was to become the first scientific investigator of the origin of the event and the extent of damage it caused. Among the many accounts collected by Suslov and Kulik are the following:

REPORTS FROM WITHIN THE AREA OF FELLED TREES

From a nomad camp on the Churgim Creek: "In Vasiliy

Dzhenkoul's nomad camp between 600 and 700 reindeer were burned, as were the reindeer dogs, all stores, and all the tepees. Luckily, Vasiliy at the time happened to be away tending another of his herds on the Ilimpo River." (5) (See location 5 on map.)

On the upper flow of the Churgim Creek: "Everything was incinerated. Only ashes remained. The storage hut of Stepan Dzhenkoul was burned, and his birch bark tepee was blown away." (6)

On the Kimchu River close to Lake Cheko: "In the nomad camp of Stepan Dzhenkoul many deer lay motionless in a stupor. All the tepees were carried away by the whirlwind." (4)

On the Kimchu River closer to Lake Cheko: "All the tepees were blown into the air; people fell unconscious." (2)

On the upper flow of the Ukagitkon River: "The herdsman S. Dronov lay unconscious for two days. His entire herd of reindeer was killed and all his household burned." (3)

On the Chamba River north of the Khavarkikta River: In the words of Ivan Aksenov: "While hunting, I was knocked to the ground unconscious and lay motionless, as if dead, then later I awoke." (11)

From the Chamba River near the Khavarkikta tributary: "In the nomadic camp of the aged hunter Lyuburman, from the family group of Shanyagir, all the tepees were felled and the old man died of shock." (12)

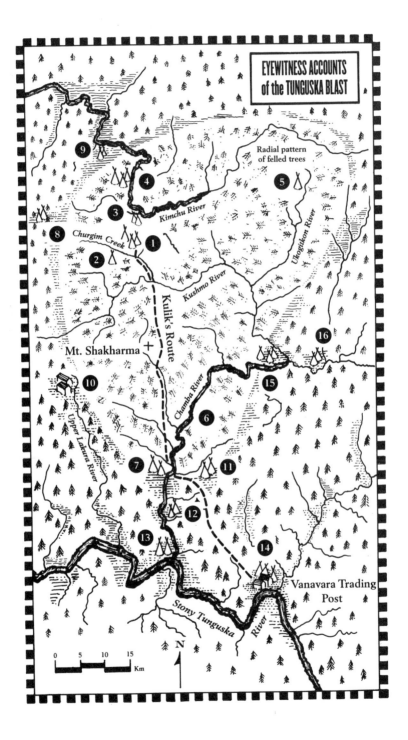

EYEWITNESS ACCOUNTS
of the TUNGUSKA BLAST

Radial pattern
of felled trees

⑨

④

③

⑤

⑧ Churgim Creek

① Kimchu River

② Kushmo River

Ukagikon River

Mt. Shakharma

Kulik's Route

⑩

⑯

⑮

Chamba River

⑥

Upper Lakura River

⑦

⑪

⑫

⑬

⑭

Vanavara Trading
Post

Stony Tunguska River

0   5   10   15
Km

N

REPORTS FROM OUTSIDE THE AREA OF FELLED TREES

Near the Chuvar Range by the upper flow of the Khushmo River: "In the nomad camp of P. Tarkichonok the reindeer herd was burned to ashes. For three days the dumbfounded people lay inert beneath blankets, as if dead." (7)

On the Kimchu River: "All the tepees were demolished, and all the storage huts were felled." (1)

From the Upper Lakura River: "All the storage shelters of S. Ankov and his three brothers were incinerated. They lost 80 sacks of flour, all their winter clothing, and stores." (13)

On the Khavarkikta River, a tributary of the Chamba River: The nomadic family group of Tungus named Machakugyr said that in their camp "the tepees were felled and the whirlwind knocked people off their feet." (14)

On the Chamba River near the lower Yakuta tributary: "The Tungus hunters Petr Doonov and his son Vasiliy were slightly contused [bruised]." (15)

At the mouth of the Chamba River: "In the nomadic camp of Pavel Aksenov, Pavel, his wives, daughter, and sons Gelencha and Pampunya were stricken with horror." (16)

The Russian researcher Yuri Kandyba, a geologist and authority on the history of the early Tunguska investigations, compiled this map showing the locations of many eyewitness accounts of the 1908 explosion of a cosmic visitor over a remote region of Tunguska in north-central Siberia. MAP BY RICK BRITTON

From the Vanavara trading post: "The sky has split apart. When the fire appeared it became so hot that one couldn't stand it. S. Semenov's shirt was as if set on fire. When the loud explosion was heard he was hurled to the ground across a distance of three sazhens [the old Russian measure of length, one sazhen is equal to 2.13 meters]. M. Kosolapov said that he felt 'as if someone had burned my ears.' A hot wind blew past us. The ground and all the huts trembled, causing the sod packing to fall from the ceilings. The glass was blasted out of the window frames. The families of P. Yakochen, M. Kosolapov and A. Kosolapov, and Marfa Bryukhanova all hid inside their huts in horror." (17)

On the Chamba River: "God in his displeasure with us tore the sky apart. In the nomad camp of Ivan Dzhenkoul all 200 reindeer in a single instant were incinerated. All of his stores of furs, food, and other goods were likewise destroyed." (8)

Near the mouth of the Khushmo River: "The tepee of Pavel Daunov was incinerated." (9)

From the Chamba River near the mouth of the Lower Dulyushma River: "Akulina was thrown up into the air as if flying. The old man Vasiliy, son of Okhchen, was thrown into the air as he slept. He flew 12 meters and was hurled into a tree, which broke his arm so that the bone was sticking out. He soon died. In a state of shock Ivan Yerineev lost his tongue. His store of two moose skins, a sack of flour, and nets was destroyed. A sack of furs became charred, and a rabbit blanket, sleeping bags, and tepee were all destroyed. The hunting dogs disappeared." (10)

According to Suslov, one had to be extremely careful in evaluating what a Tungus tribesman reported had happened. This was especially so if an account bordered on the supernatural, or appeared to come from that fuzzy state of mind somewhere between consciousness and unconsciousness. From June 1 through June 4, 1926 Suslov interviewed sixty Tungus hunters in the village of Strelka on the Chunya River 150 kilometers north of Vanavara. General agreement among all those he interviewed convinced him that the eyewitness accounts he collected were reliable and not a product of invention. First, certain expressions occurred over and over again from one eyewitness to the next: "The dogs were killed"; "the reindeer were annihilated"; and "the forest was crushed." Second, the accounts of Lyuchetkan, Akulina, and others were verified independently by many of those interviewed. During a group interview with several hunters, all agreed about the details of the firestorm: it had slammed into the riverbank near the point where the Khushma River flows into the Chamba River. Then it incinerated 200 reindeer belonging to Stepan Ilich Onkoul of the Kurkagyr tribe and demolished all his storehouses of food and supplies.

KULIK INTERVIEWS EYEWITNESSES

In his initial report to the Soviet Academy of Sciences about his visit to the Tunguska area ("The Problem of the Impact Area of the Tunguska Meteorite of 1908") Kulik relates a number of his interviews with eyewitnesses. Like Suslov, he also was convinced of the authenticity of the accounts. For example, the report about S. Semenov and his burning shirt (see page 14) was confirmed and elaborated by Semenov himself: "The explosion occurred about eight o'clock in the morning. I was

Kulik, as photographed in November 1928, probably by Suslov. Kulik wears a typical goatskin coat and is armed for possible encounters with bears or wolves.
COURTESY: COMMITTEE ON METEORITES, RUSSIAN ACADEMY OF SCIENCES

then living in the trading post of Vanavara, located on the Stony Tunguska River. At the time I was resting from repairing my building. From my porch, off to the northwest there was a great flash of light soon followed by heat so intense that I could not remain on the porch, and my shirt felt as if it were burning on my back. A large fireball filled much of the sky, and then it grew dark. I felt an explosion so strong that it knocked me about two meters across the ground, where I lost consciousness. When I came to a few moments later I could still hear the loud sound from the explosion, and the house was shaking so violently that I thought it would be knocked off its foundation."

On April 16, 1927 Kulik interviewed Lyuchetkan, who said that the epicenter of the blast seemed to have been over the grazing and browsing region of the Evenki hunter Vasiliy Ilich. Evenki "wealth" was measured in the size of their reindeer herds. Vasiliy, owner of some 1,500 of the animals, was considered among the wealthiest. He also kept a number of storehouses filled with harnesses for the reindeer, clothing, furs, food stores, and other household goods. The firestorm incinerated all the animals and stores alike. When Lyuchetkan's brothers Burucha and Mugocha later roamed over the area in search of any of their own surviving reindeer and stores, they found only charred carcasses. Samovars, dishes, and cooking utensils all had been melted by the fierce heat.

The Evenki hunters, along with Russian fur traders, told Kulik that the region of felled trees formed a fan-shaped pattern and that the treetops lay pointing outward from the central epicenter area of the blast. A specialist in meteoric science, Kulik was puzzled by a number of unusual things. He felt that perhaps the outstanding irregularity was the inescapable fact that a tremendous firestorm had accompanied a meteorite as it plunged into Earth's atmosphere, or that the firestorm resulted from the meteorite's explosion. Try as he might, he could not satisfactorily explain the firestorm. Twenty years later, on February 12, 1947, over the mountainous region of eastern Siberia near Vladivostok, the largest meteorite of this century burst and fragmented before its many pieces struck the ground, but it neither flattened the surrounding forest nor brought with it a destructive firestorm. Kulik believed that the 1908 cosmic visitor was also unusual both in its mass and in its speed of entry into the atmosphere.

Among his report's concluding remarks to the Academy was the statement: "A more detailed investigation of the fall region is essential."

CHAPTER THREE

The
"SLEEPING LAND"

*T*he Tunguska event is remarkable for the small loss of human life caused by the greatest known explosion in the history of civilization, including the 1883 blowout of the volcanic mountain-island of Krakatoa, near Java and Sumatra. On August 26 of that year the mountain of Krakatoa began rumbling and erupting in a series of explosions, and then the following day there was one mighty blast of flame, smoke, and ash. When the sea calmed and the air cleared, there was nothing. The mountain had vanished. It had once towered 800 meters above the waves but had plunged to a depth of 275 meters below the ocean's surface. The noise from the explosion was heard 2,750 kilometers away in Australia. Churned up by the eruption, the sea rose in a gigantic wave that crashed down on the coastal villages of Java and Sumatra killing 36,500 people. But the Tunguska blast was mightier.

The same year the cosmic visitor exploded over Tunguska, an unrelated earthquake devastated the Italian cities of Messina and Reggio, and took 100,000 human lives. Many of the victims were trapped in narrow streets when poorly constructed buildings toppled down on them. In 1920 an earthquake in Kansu,

China killed some 200,000 people. In 1939 about 300,000 people died when an earthquake shook Concepción, Chile. That same year central Turkey was also struck by an earthquake. Some 50,000 perished. As Academician Vasiliev suggested in the Preface, had the Tunguska blast occurred over one of the world's major cities, the death toll could have approached the total of the five catastrophes just cited.

The Tunguska event may seem remarkable for the only two reported human lives it claimed. But it might seem even more remarkable for the long silence—from 1908 to 1921—on the part of the international scientific community, which showed no interest in investigating the incident. This is especially so considering the "light nights" observed by thousands across Europe and Asia, and the seismic and atmospheric disturbances recorded around the globe. If there is a credible excuse for inaction on the part of the international scientific community, it can be attributed to a fundamental characteristic of Tunguska—its remoteness.

A LAND OF ETERNAL FROST

For more than 400 years since Russia began to occupy the Siberian wilderness, the gigantic region has remained remote. But it is less so now than when it took a year to cross its broad expanse by horse and boat. Siberia, from a Tartar word meaning "sleeping land," is a vast region only slightly smaller than the United States. Lacking precise geographic boundaries, Siberia extends eastward across northern Asia from the Ural Mountains to the Pacific Ocean. It borders the Arctic Ocean in the north and sprawls southward, first across the tundra, then through the great taiga forest zone, and finally over the steppes of Central Asia to the northern borders of Kasakhstan and Mongolia.

To this day, transportation within the region remains poor. There are no roads to Vanavara, for example. You get there on foot, by river, or by air. North-south traffic is served by the Lena, Ob, and Yenisei rivers and their thousands of tributaries. East-west traffic is by the Trans-Siberian Railroad, completed three years before the Tunguska explosion. Dissidents, political prisoners, and criminals of every description traditionally have been shipped off to Siberian penal colonies—including Stalin's notorious Gulags—or exiled to remote villages. Lenin was exiled to Siberia, as was Trotsky. So was Stalin, and most likely at the very time of the Tunguska event. Most of the political prisoners, dissidents, and their descendants were simply abandoned in that vast empty land. Since there was no easy or reliable means of escape, they had no choice but to follow the wish of the government to settle and help tame the inhospitable wilderness.

Lenin's study in a small Siberian village where he was exiled just before the October revolution.   Photo by Gallant

Three quarters of Siberia is a land of "eternal frost," or permafrost, a crust of ice, bog, and soil frozen to a depth of some 300 meters on the average. In places the frost penetrates to a depth of 1,500 meters! Despite heat welling up from Earth's interior and heat from the summer Sun, the permafrost temperature remains a constant -4 degrees Celsius. Only during a few weeks of summer does it melt to a depth of a few feet.

According to Canadian writer Farley Mowat:

> Anything which disturbs the delicate temperature balance protecting permafrost can bring about a horrendous change. A tracked vehicle grading over summer tundra and breaking through the thin insulating layer of moss and lichen can create vast, heaving ditches which will endure for centuries. Casual damage to the forest floor during timbering operations can cause a fatal thaw which leaves the shallow-rooted trees with no hold on anything but quaking bog, and finally sends them toppling into chaos. And structures built by man can, through the slight temperature rise created by their own weight, or by heat radiated from them, create a local swamp into which the buildings sink, totter and collapse. The same thing can happen to roads, or in fact to anything man tries to build upon the frozen ground.

To get some feeling for this enormous land on my way to the 1992 Tunguska expedition, I chose not to fly the 4,000 kilometers from Moscow to Krasnoyarsk. Instead, I realized a dream I had had since my teens on reading works of Tolstoy, Dostoyevsky, and Chekhov. That dream was to travel on the Trans-Siberian Railroad. The Russian novelist Anton Chekhov's moving and graphic descriptions of his three-month crossing of Siberia in 1890, first by horse and carriage and then by steamer, had made me long to see Siberia from the ground rather than from the indifferent perspective of an airplane. I wanted to experience the texture of the land from within its fabric, not above it, to sense its aromas, and to mix among its peoples and to hear them speak.

CLOUD MERCHANTS AND WET FENCES

On April 29, 1890, while sailing on the river Kama, Chekhov wrote to his family that "the banks are bare, the trees bare, the earth a mat-brown, patches of snow stretch ahead and the wind is such that even the devil himself couldn't blow as sharply or unpleasantly. When the cold wind blows and ripples the water, which after the spring's flooding has taken on the color of coffee slops, everything turns cold and lonely and wretched; the accordion sounds on the shore seem mournful and the figures in torn sheepskin coats standing motionless on the barges we encounter appear permanently stiff with sorrow. The cities of the Kama are gray; it looks as though their inhabitants occupied themselves exclusively in the manufacture of lowering clouds, boredom, wet fences and street filth."

From the town of Ekaterinburg Chekhov wrote: "The people here inspire the newcomer with something like horror; they are high-cheekboned, with jutting foreheads, broad-shouldered, have little eyes and enormously big fists." Chekhov wrote of a three-inch snowfall on May 14, of a "superabundance" of ducks—"I could have shot a thousand of them in one day"—of penniless vagrants wandering about with "pots on their backs," and of tramps so destitute that they would murder a woman peasant for want of the cloth of her skirt. When Chekhov saw those Siberian people known as Tartars, and heard them described by local people, he wrote his family: "My God! How rich Russia is in good people! If it were not for the cold which deprives Siberia of summer, and were it not for the officials who corrupt the peasants and exiles, Siberia would be the very richest and happiest of territories." On arriving at Krasnoyarsk he referred to the world's most voluminous river, the Yenisei, as "that fierce and mighty warrior." I was to spend eleven days on that fierce and mighty warrior aboard the ship *Anton Chekhov* as it carried me north into the Kara Sea of the southern Arctic Ocean and the outpost of Dickson at 73 degrees north latitude. That is north of Norway, north of Alaska, halfway up Greenland. Even in August you can expect to encounter ice floes if the wind is right.

The train sped me on a three-day warm July journey across some of the most beautiful country I have ever seen—across the Urals, through forests of pine, cedar, spruce, and larch, across

Dachas by the tens and hundreds pepper the countryside around cities and large towns. A "dacha" is a tiny camp on a small plot of land intensively farmed for vegetables, fruit, and berries to provide the average Russian family with food otherwise too expensive on the open market, or not even available. Six dachas are seen here.   PHOTO BY GALLANT

seemingly endless expanses of broad and flat fields adorned
with little islands of silver birches gleaming pink in the early
morning sun, then shining intensely white at noon, and a ghostly gray by moonlight. On crossing the steppes of Central Asia I
almost expected to see giraffes and lions in the distance, so similar is this land to the African Savanna. When Chekhov crossed
these fields a century and two years earlier, they were snow covered, and ice choked the rivers and streams. As we approached
villages both sides of the tracks suddenly became vegetable gar-
dens with small plots of potatoes being worked by husky female
peasants who seldom looked up from their hoes. From time to
time the train slowed to a crawl as we passed a tiny wooden hut
with a man or woman standing just outside the entrance and
holding either a plain yellow or red circular sign. These were
signals to the engineer announcing whether the tracks ahead
were clear (yellow) or not (red). An electronically operated sig-
nal system for the railroad has yet to come to Siberia.

The importance of the Trans-Siberian Railroad as the principal means of east-west travel was driven home to me by the
frequency of other passenger or freight trains passing us in the
opposite direction. Before arriving at Novosibirsk, from which
you would drop straight into China if you slid due south down
the map, we were delayed for an hour by the wave of a red sign.
You learn not to ask why the delay; no one ever knows. During
that hour I counted eighteen trains passing us westbound. They
carried people, logs, milled boards, tanks of natural gas, military
tanks, tractors, trucks, more tractors, marble chips, drilling
equipment, military vehicles of all sizes and sorts, containers
closed and banded and locked, and endless cars of coal, coal,
and more coal. The variety of the Siberian landscape matches
the richness of its natural resources—vast quantities of oil, natural gas, coal, iron ore, gold, platinum, nickel, timber, and
gemstones galore, some so rare that they are found only at a single site in Siberia.

We were five hours late when we arrived at the Novosibirsk station at 4:00 A.M. I wished I had been traveling with Chekhov. At every stop, day or night, peasant women appeared out of nowhere displaying a variety of food for sale for ten, twenty, thirty roubles—nickels and dimes. At Mareensk we were met by shawled women with kerchiefs over their heads, their faces wrinkled by the elements and lined by age. Their hands, extended with their offerings, were calloused and often deformed by arthritis or hard work. They were selling cabbage pies, steaming boiled potatoes, radishes, raspberries, and blueberries. Our next stop, and for me the last, was Krasnoyarsk, although the train was to continue on for several more days to its final destination, China's capital of Beijing. The engineer had neither gained nor lost a minute over the 550 kilometers from Novosibirsk. At Krasnoyarsk we were still exactly five hours late.

THE SIBERIAN TAIGA

Northward some 600 or more kilometers from the Trans-Siberian rail line is the densest region of the taiga and tundra environment, with swamps and bogs in every direction. Even as late as mid-June the tundra remains frozen to an arm's depth beneath the downy surface. One Russian writer, Yuri Semyonov, has described the region as a "sinister" land where "the weak and imprudent often perish . . . where everything below is decayed and rotten, and everything above withered, where only the corpses of the huge trunks slowly moulder away in the brackish water." Mosquitoes here are reputed to be the fiercest, largest, and most numerous of any place in the world. The Russians call them "flying alligators." The only protection against them is heavy clothing, gloves, and a "helmet" of netting to protect your face and head. Chemical repellents are useless. The mosquitoes just laugh.

This, then, was the remote and inhospitable land that the legendary hero of the search for the Tunguska object, Leonid A. Kulik, was to make his temporary home at various times over a period of nearly twenty years, even during the fierce Siberian winter. And it was the place I was to make my temporary home. But Kulik does not enter our story, at least as the Tunguska event's principal investigator, until 1921. How, you may again ask, could an event so calamitous, so terrifying to the thousands who were shaken by it, go uninvestigated for so many years?

CHAPTER FOUR

The FIRST

"EXPEDITION"

to the

EPICENTER'S EDGE

*T*he superstitions of the Tungus people and their links with the spirit world through their shamans were to keep them away from the "enchanted" land; that is, the epicenter region where the forest had been seared and flattened by the fire-wind. Only the most courageous among the Tungus nomad hunters, or the foolish, were to enter the sacred land and gaze on the results of Ogdy's wrath. And "sinister" events, according to more than one observer, were to claim the lives of at least two.

We will now move ahead from 1908, the year of the explosion, to 1910. Kulik, then twenty-seven years old, was in prison for revolutionary activities and was to remain under the eye of government police for two years. Born on August 31, 1883 in Tartu, Estonia, he completed studies at St. Petersburg's Forestry Institute and then studied mathematics and physics at Kazan University. Four years before the 1908 explosion he had fought in the Russo-Japanese War, which ended the following year in Russia's humiliating defeat. In 1910 Kulik knew nothing about the Tunguska event and was several thousand kilometers away in St. Petersburg.

Kulik, as photographed in 1916 as a junior officer in the army of Czar Nicholas II of Russia

COURTESY: COMMITTEE ON METEORITES, RUSSIAN ACADEMY OF SCIENCES

But closer to the event, in Vanavara and in villages along the Angara River, political prisoners living in exile developed a scientific curiosity about the explosion. Most of these political prisoners and other educated Russians who knew about the event generally supposed that a large meteorite had fallen. The Russian merchants who bought furs of sable, bear, fox, and moose from the Tungus hunters had a more practical interest in the event, especially a man by the name of Susdalev, the wealthiest and most influential merchant among them.

SUSDALEV'S PLAN

My companion and guide during the 1992 expedition, Yuriy Kandyba, an authority on the early history of the Tunguska expeditions, told me about Susdalev one afternoon while we were evading mosquitoes by ducking in and out of the smoke of our campfire at Kulik's base lodge. Susdalev had designed a clever plan to become even richer and gain additional influence over the Tungus people by playing on their superstitious nature.

The idea was to keep the Russian merchants in the region away from the meteorite site. An effective way to do this was to keep the Tungus away from the site also, so that they would have no furs to trade with the Russians. Earlier, the Russian merchants had driven a number of Tungus tribes off their best reindeer pasture land because the Russians knew the area had rich gold deposits and they did not want the Tungus people to mine the gold. So the Tungus were restricted to less favored land closer to the epicenter region. Now the epicenter region itself was about to be placed off limits to them, at least temporarily and until Susdalev gained control.

His scheme included getting the most influential Tungus leaders to keep their own people away from the meteorite site. To set his plan in motion, Susdalev persuaded the most clever Tungus he knew, Ivan Aksenov, to lead a small party to the edge of the epicenter, or at least to the point where Aksenov thought the epicenter region began. In addition to Aksenov, the party included the leaders of several family tribes and a number of the most powerful shamans. Eventually they arrived at a lake, which Aksenov said had been formed by the Tunguska "meteorite." Susdalev was satisfied that they had come far enough. He felt sure that they stood at the edge of the region devastated by Ogdy's fire, for before him, and to a great distance, he saw huge trees felled and lying like matches arranged in straight lines. He instructed several of the Tungus to plant a huge spruce pole firmly in the ground. Then, as planned, he signaled the shamans. They began to sing songs that officially proclaimed the devastated area as sacred, or "enchanted." In short, a taboo that said "No Trespassing" had been put in effect. For many years thereafter the only people to enter the epicenter area were the relatives of those Tungus who had pastured their reindeer herds in the area before the great fireball came down.

According to Kandyba, the Susdalev group's journey to the edge of the epicenter region can be regarded as the first "expedition" to the site. When I asked him if this incident had ever been published before, he said "not to my knowledge."

KULIK FINDS A FRIEND

After his two years under police surveillance, Kulik was sent to the Ural Mountains where he worked as a forestry official. While there he happened to meet a small expedition of geologists searching for mineral deposits. The group's leader, who was to become Kulik's friend and idol, was the highly respected geochemist and mineralogist Vladimir Vernadsky. Vernadsky took to the younger man, admiring his personality and so respecting his quick grasp of mineralogy that he predicted Kulik would one day make a place for himself as a major scientific researcher. Vernadsky arranged for Kulik to be assigned to his expedition. Kulik's next stroke of good fortune was to be offered a position in St. Petersburg's prestigious Mineralogical Museum of the Academy of Sciences. His wife, Lydia Ivanova, worked with him there.

In 1914 Kulik found himself fighting yet another war when he was drafted to fight in World War I. After Russia's defeat, he returned to his museum post. The year 1917 found him on another expedition in the Urals. While there, news reached him about a momentous event—the October Revolution—that was to steer Russia into a new era of history. It marked the end of Russia's nobility and their rule over the country. Finding himself cut off by the war from Petrograd, the new name for St. Petersburg, Kulik set out eastward for Tomsk, Siberia's major city 500 kilometers west of Krasnoyarsk. For the next three years he taught mineralogy at Tomsk University.

The year 1920 found him back in his museum post in Petrograd, where he began an intensive study of meteorites. Just as Vernadsky had taken an instant liking to Kulik, so did another highly respected mineralogist and authority on meteorites, E. L. Krinov. Krinov admired Kulik not only for his quick mind and abilities as a researcher, but also for his determination and courage to express and defend unpopular views. In a short time Kulik had established himself as one of the leading authorities on meteorites. His new interest and expertise spurred him to collect for and enlarge the museum's national collection of meteorites. At the time Kulik had no idea that his newly acquired interest would launch him on a search that would consume his mind and soul for the rest of his life.

By Kulik's time the study of meteorites had advanced enough so that it was common knowledge that meteorites come from space, rather than originating at Earth's surface or within the atmosphere, as had been believed into the 1800s. The very name "meteorite," which derives from a Greek root word *meteorors* (meaning "high in the air"), reflects the earlier fuzzy view that meteorites were most likely products of the atmosphere. Scientists of the famous French Academy of Sciences mocked the notion that meteorites came from outer space. Similarly the United States' only scientist-president, Thomas Jefferson, ridiculed the idea of "stones from space falling on Earth." But on April 26, 1803, a fireball meteorite exploded over L'Aigle, France, and two months later was investigated by Jean B. Biot. He succeeded in convincing scientists that meteorites did, indeed, fall from space. On examining the composition of many specimens of the fall he was able to show that the fragments could not have originated from anywhere around L'Aigle. It was to Biot's credit that the serious study of meteorites was begun.

WHERE METEORITES COME FROM

Between the orbits of Mars and Jupiter are millions of pieces of rock and metal called asteroids, which we will examine more closely in the last chapter. When asteroids from time to time smash into each other they shatter into many smaller pieces. These smaller pieces fly off into new orbits that take them on paths that cross the orbits of the planets. We call these bits and pieces of smashed asteroids "meteoroids" when they are in space.

Meteoroids enter Earth's air at speeds of about 15 to 70 kilometers per second. Their high speed creates friction with the atmosphere, and they burn and flare up as brief streaks of light we call "meteors." If a meteoroid survives its blazing journey down through the air and hits the ground, it is called a "meteorite." Some are made of rock (silicate) and are called *stony* meteorites. Others are made of metal (iron and nickel) and are called *iron* meteorites. And still others are part rock and part metal and are called *stony-irons*.

Before astronomers discovered where meteorites come from, many people thought they were stars falling out of the sky. You still hear the terms "falling stars" and "shooting stars." On a clear night away from the glare of city lights, you can see about five meteors an hour. Meteor dust rains down through Earth's air every day, and tons of tiny meteorites, called "micrometeorites," fall to the ground each day.

You may be wondering: Has anyone ever been struck and killed by a meteorite? There are many such claims. During almost every month of the year, we have one or more meteor showers. Shower meteors are the remains of old burned-out comets that cross Earth's orbit in swarms with the regularity of a Japanese train. During an especially active shower you can

The Willamette meteorite, on display at the American Museum–Hayden Planetarium in New York City, is the remains of a meteoroid that was sculpted by frictional heating as it blazed through Earth's atmosphere. It is solid iron and weighs 14.5 tons. It measures about three meters from end to end and was found in Oregon in 1902.   COURTESY: THE AMERICAN MUSEUM–HAYDEN PLANETARIUM

Deadly showers of stones are the stuff of legends—as depicted in this 16th-century woodcut. Numerous reports chronicle human deaths by meteoric strikes.
ILLUSTRATION FROM CONRAD LYCOSTHENES' CHRONICLES OF PRODIGIES (1557)

expect to see about 50 meteors an hour. A report in the journal *Meteoritics* (November 1994) mentions an especially severe meteor shower in the year 1490 over Ch'ing-yang in China's Shansi Province that allegedly killed more than 10,000 people. The journal *Meteorite!* (February 1995) reports that a meteorite that was blasted off the surface of Mars penetrated Earth's atmosphere over the Egyptian town of Nakhla killing a dog—"the only authenticated case of an Earthling being killed by a Martian," according to the report.

The largest known meteorite, called the Hoba West, fell on Botswana, in southern Africa, well over 10,000 years ago. It weighs some 60 tons, about as heavy as twenty pickup trucks, but is estimated to have weighed closer to 100 tons when it fell. Much of the iron meteorite, along with all its original crater, has eroded over the many centuries.

The second largest known meteorite is Ahnighito, another iron that weighs about 34 tons. "Ahnighito" is an Eskimo word meaning "tent," chosen for the meteorite's size and shape. Found in Cape York, Greenland, it was shipped to New York City by Admiral Peary in 1897 and today is on display in The American Museum of Natural History. Interestingly, Ahnighito was one of four irons belonging to the same fall.

About 50,000 years ago a small asteroid about the size of a railroad car crashed into the Arizona desert and blasted out a crater almost 1.6 kilometers in diameter and nearly 180 meters deep. Yet the "meteorite" that Kulik was to spend years searching for was larger than any of these: It was an object presumed to be about 1,700 times more massive than any previously known on Earth!

KULIK'S SEARCH
BEGINS

*O*ne day a colleague showed Kulik an old newspaper account of a reported meteorite fall in the Tomsk region not far from the Filimonovo junction on the Trans-Siberian railway line. According to the story, the meteorite was large enough to have set up a "frightful roar and a deafening crash." It reportedly fell in late June 1908, around 8:00 A.M.

Kulik's first reaction must have been surprise and possibly a touch of disbelief. Why had he not heard of this seemingly impressive event when he had taught mineralogy at Tomsk University? He read on. So curious was the engineer of a passenger train arriving at the junction when the meteorite reportedly struck that he stopped the train. Equally curious, the passengers climbed out to see what had happened. According to the story, they "were unable to study the meteorite closely because it was red hot" and had nearly buried itself in the ground. Later, the story went on, the meteorite cooled enough to be closely examined. It was said to be a whitish stone block about the size of a large chair.

Kulik was fascinated by the story (which turned out to be almost entirely false). Thorough investigator that he was, he immediately began searching through summer issues of Siberian newspapers published in 1908 from the Tomsk and Krasnoyarsk regions. To his surprise he found account after account of a catastrophic explosion in June 1908, although there often were disagreements in certain details. Kulik's instincts told him that he was on to something important, quite possibly a grandaddy meteorite that would prove valuable to their scientific study.

OTHER ACCOUNTS OF A 1908 BLAST

One such story that Kulik most likely saw appeared in the newspaper *Krasnoyarian* for July 13, 1908:

> From the village of Kezhemskoye: An unusual phenomenon was noticed in this region at 7:43 A.M. near the beginning of this month (July). A loud noise was heard as if caused by a strong wind. After that came a terrible noise accompanied by an underground shock that caused buildings to tremble. The impression was that someone hit the building severely with some huge log or a heavy stone.
>
> After the first shock, a second one of the same strength followed, and then a third. The interval between the first and third shocks was accompanied by an unusual underground noise that sounded like a dozen trains rattling the rails simultaneously. The next five to six minutes sounded like a long volley of about 50 to 60 artillery bursts at short and nearly equal intervals. Gradually the shocks weakened.
>
> A minute and a half or two minutes after the cannonade, there were six more shocks like a distant cannonade, yet clearly heard and accompanied by a

trembling of the earth that could be distinctly felt. At first glance the sky seemed absolutely clear. There was no wind, no clouds. But a more careful look revealed in the north—that is, from the direction where the noise seemed to come—something that looked like a cloud and had the color of ash. Gradually it became smaller and more and more transparent. By two o'clock in the afternoon it had disappeared.

This very phenomenon, according to information received so far, was also observed at the same strength in nearby villages up and down the Angara River, at a distance of 300 versts [about 320 kilometers] in both directions from Kezhemskoye. In some locations glass was broken out of the window frames. How strong the first shocks were you can judge by some cases of horses and people being knocked off their feet.

According to eyewitnesses, before the first shocks were heard, the sky was split from south to north by what appeared to be a celestial body of fire which veered slightly to the northeast; but because of its speed, and especially the suddenness of its appearance, nobody noticed either its size or shape. But in many and different villages people observing the path of the flying object distinctly saw a giant fire blaze up when the object appeared to touch the horizon. And the ash-colored cloud, mentioned above, was later observed in that spot. But the fiery outburst was seen to occur much lower than the cloud, at the level of the forest treetops, and was so great that it split the sky apart.

The blaze was so strong that it was reflected in most rooms that faced north. This reflected glare was so strong that the guards of the *volost* offices [the smallest administrative division of tsarist Russia] reported seeing it. The blaze must have lasted for at least a minute, because it was noticed by many peasants in the fields. As soon as the fire had gone, the shocks were heard. One could feel in the ominous silence between shocks that some very unusual phenomenon of nature was occurring. On the island near the village the cows and horses became noisy and began running from one shore to the other. One had a feeling that the earth would split apart in a moment and everything would fall into an abyss. Terrible shocks were heard coming from somewhere. They shook the air, and their unknown source inspired superstitious awe. One literally became dumbfounded.

The following story appeared in the *Tomsk Diocesan News* for September 1, 1908. The story had the headline, THE SUNSET OF THE 30TH OF JUNE:

The light sunsets observed on the nights of the 29th and 30th of June and the 1st of July were seen over a vast territory. They were observed from the parallel of St. Petersburg to the Black Sea, also in Germany. The displays being the northern lights can be ruled out because they were not accompanied by magnetic disturbances.

Dr. V. F. Nagorny reported that while on his way from Kineshma to Nizhniy Novgorod on the Volga River he had seen that the left edge of the light strip had the definite shape of the reversed Cyrillic letter "3" against the dark background of the clear sky, where the Moon was low. Besides the illuminated area, or spot, there were horizontal light and dark stripes, although with very little contrast. This suggests that in very high layers of the atmosphere there were thin clouds of dust being brightly illuminated by the Sun, as occurred in the case of the volcano Krakatoa in 1883.

A special effect [also was observed] in southern latitudes. Usually at the time such effects are seen the sky is absolutely dark, but on the 30th of June it was so light that one could read [a newspaper]. In many places people noticed that objects cast shadows. In Taganrog the ships anchored in the harbor could be seen at a distance of 300 to 400 sazhens [about 750 meters].

The following appeared in the newspaper *The Trading-Industrial Gazette SPB* of St. Petersburg for July 3, 1908: "BERLIN, July 1: Berlin, Copenhagen, Kenigsberg, and along the whole coast of the Baltic Sea unusually yellow and beautiful lights were observed in the northern sky, reminding one of the Krakotoa explosion of 1883."

The following day the same paper ran a story headlined: "MORE ABOUT THE FALL OF THE METEORITE: YESTERDAY WE RECEIVED A TELEGRAM SAYING ONLY—'THE NOISE WAS CONSIDERABLE, BUT NO STONE FELL.'"

A story published in the Irkutsk paper *Sibir* on July 2 reported eyewitness accounts of people living in the village of Nizhne-Karelinsk about 500 kilometers southeast of Vanavara: "All the inhabitants of the village ran out into the street in panic. The old women wept, everyone thought that the end of the world was approaching." The people had seen a body shining blindingly bright, and moments later a large cloud of black smoke arising from where the bluish-white light exploded. The story went on to describe the explosion as sounding like gunfire and shaking all the buildings.

A few days after the June 30 blast a Tomsk newspaper sent one of its reporters to Kansk, which had become the source of many descriptions, and rumors, of the explosion. At this stage no one, except a handful of Tungus hunters, knew the approximate location of the cosmic catastrophe. The reporter was told that from Kansk "the noise was considerable, but no stones fell" on the area. The paper took the position that what had rocked Kansk most likely had been an earthquake that produced "a subterranean crash and a roar" that rattled a large area. "Five to seven minutes later a second crash followed, louder than the first, accompanied by a similar roar and followed after a brief interval by yet another crash."

The more Kulik read of such accounts, the harder he found it to rule out a meteorite fall, although his skills as a scientific investigator cautioned him against rushing to conclusions. For example, meteors almost always are observed only at night—unless they are exceptionally large ones called "bolides." And he knew of no instances when a meteorite fall had started raging fires, as must have been the case of the 1908 explosion that produced an enormous cloud of ash and dust reminiscent of the mighty Krakatoa blast. But what if this meteorite had been a monster one, larger than any that had ever collided with Earth in human history, larger than anything scientists had ever had the opportunity to study? he wondered. He was convinced that he was about to become involved in what has since been commonly called the "cosmic mystery of the century."

But at this stage he didn't even know where the object had fallen. Visual reports of it came from a huge area, larger than France, extending over some 800 kilometers, and reports of its thunder came from even farther away. Where to begin his search?

A METEORITE TREASURE?

Here we should pause to recount the stroke of good luck that enabled Kulik to head an expedition to search for meteorites on behalf of his government—a search that he was able to direct toward the 1908 mystery object.

The Russians' search for the meteorite that exploded over central Siberia in 1908 was spurred by reports of a large meteorite discovered buried beneath the southern rim of the Meteor Crater in Arizona. The floor of the crater is as deep as a six-story building and the size of a cluster of fifteen football fields. The Arizona meteorite was reported to be more than 90 percent iron, 6 percent nickel, and contained smaller amounts of the precious metals platinum and iridium.

AMERICAN MUSEUM OF NATURAL HISTORY

In the early 1900s American industrial prospectors from Philadelphia decided to drill into the floor of Meteor Crater in Arizona in expectation of striking it rich. Although they had high hopes of finding and mining the buried body of the huge meteorite, they failed to locate the mass of metal. Several years later, another mining exploration company did locate the meteorite when they drilled to a depth of 420 meters beneath the southern rim of the gigantic hole. The floor of the crater was as deep as a six-story building is high and was the size of a cluster of about fifteen football fields. Although the prospectors found the cosmic missile, they decided it was too difficult to mine. Samples of the object suggested that it was more than 90 percent iron, 6 percent nickel, and contained smaller amounts of the precious metals platinum and iridium.

The Russian scientific community surely must have been aware of the goings on in Arizona, and possibly they began to consider similarly exploiting their own meteorite treasures. The location of numerous meteorite falls in many parts of the then Soviet Union had been dutifully recorded over the years, and the Tunguska object might turn out to be an even richer source of money much needed by the new four-year-old Soviet government. So the Soviet Academy of Sciences decided to organize an expedition, the purpose of which would be "to study the places and circumstances in which meteorites had fallen and been found at various times, and to collect information about them from the local populations," according to Kulik's colleague, Krinov. The logical person to head such an expedition was the thirty-eight-year-old Kulik, of the Academy's very own Mineralogical Museum.

It was during the time Kulik was preparing for the 1921 expedition that a colleague had called his attention to the bogus report of the Tomsk meteorite fall. What interested Kulik almost as much as the event itself was that not a single scientific expedition had yet been sent to search for the site of the explosion. Here was an opportunity of a lifetime, made possible by his friend Vernadsky, who had persuaded the Academy to finance the expedition.

DISAPPOINTMENT AND HOPE

As his departure time of September 5 neared, Kulik's excitement mounted. His plan was to proceed to Kansk to interview people who had witnessed the grand explosion of 1908, which Kulik had come to refer to as the "Filimonovo meteorite." He hoped that interviews with eyewitnesses would put him on the trail of the actual fall point.

On the Trans-Siberian Railroad Kulik's small group had its own private railway car for equipment and supplies. After departing from Petrograd and stopping at Moscow, the train crossed the Urals, entered the steppe region, and stopped at Omsk just north of Kazakhstan. It also stopped at Kulik's university city of Tomsk, then Krasnoyarsk, and finally arrived at Kansk.

Kulik lost no time in seeking out eyewitnesses who could describe what they saw and heard on the morning of June 30, 1908. He also distributed a questionnaire to people in Kansk and outlying areas, which brought additional accounts of the blast. Most of the reports were vivid and rich in detail. They described the luminous sky, the thunderous explosions, and the shaking ground. Kulik also learned that investigators from Tomsk and Irkutsk, who had visited Kansk soon after the explosion, had failed to find any sign of the "Filimonovo meteorite." Disappointed, Kulik concluded that the fireball and "meteorite" had struck farther to the north, most likely in the region of the Podkamennaya (Stony) Tunguska River. But there was not time to embark on an extended expedition, which would require further financing, technical equipment that he did not have then, supplies, and workers.

On his return to Petrograd, Kulik wrote his report to the Academy. True to his nature, he firmly expressed his opinion that the fireball explosion had been a large meteorite in a cocoon of "burning gases." He finished the report with a sting:

The Tunguska fire storm was the first known example of such an event in human history. It must be investigated!

And Kulik was specific in what he knew had to be done: (1) Photographs of the entire area of destruction must be taken from the air to determine the most promising points to excavate for the meteorite; (2) A magnetic survey of the "crater area" should also be made.

CHAPTER SIX

The FIRST
EXPEDITION, *and a*
SHAMAN'S TALE

Despite his appeals to the Academy, Kulik's request to search for the epicenter of the explosion was not approved until 1927. Meanwhile he continued to gather eyewitness accounts and eagerly read reports of Russian scientists who had visited the areas of Kansk and Vanavara.

For example, in 1924, the geologist S. V. Obruchev was doing research near Vanavara along the Stony Tunguska River. The Tungus' show of fear at the mention of the event seemed a clue that he might be in or near the region of the 1908 explosion. In a letter to Kulik he reported that "in the eyes of the Tungus people, the meteorite is apparently sacred, and they carefully conceal the place where it fell." One Tungus, however, told him that several days northeast of Vanavara was a vast region of "flattened forest," and that no one was permitted to go there, especially outsiders. Like Kulik, Obruchev felt that the object probably was a gigantic meteorite. During the previous year another geologist named Sobolev, who also had been doing research in the area, sent to Kulik Lyuchetkan's graphic account of his brothers' loss of their reindeer herds, stores, and tepees.

In 1926, from the first to the fourth of June, the ethnographer Suslov collected some sixty eyewitness accounts of the blast, which soon afterward were brought to Kulik's attention. At first Suslov could not be sure about the reliability of what the Evenki people told him, but the more he listened to their accounts, the more he believed them. While truthfulness was one of Suslov's concerns about the reliability of eyewitness accounts, the Tungus' perception of what actually had occurred was another. For instance,   Kosolapova, the daughter of Semenov, whom Kulik interviewed, who was nineteen at the time of the blast, recalled what she "saw" in these words: "Suddenly before me I saw the sky in the north open to the ground and fire poured out. We were terrified, but the sky closed again."

A FLIGHT PATH FOR THE COSMIC VISITOR

About the time Suslov was interviewing Evenki eyewitnesses, a researcher named V. Voznesensky was trying to trace the flight path of the 1908 object and its fall point. He had been the director of the Irkutsk Magnetic and Meteorological Observatory and so had access to all of its earthquake tremor records. He also studied the growing body of information that Kulik had been collecting and that had been brought to light by Obruchev. The task he set himself was to piece together all that material with the numerous sightings from far southern Siberia northward to the general area of the blast. Also to be included as part of the picture were the reports of "thunder," rumblings, and the final cannonade of blasts when the object detonated. He felt that he could then draw a map suggesting a possible flight path of the object, its approximate fall point, and the epicenter area of forest devastation. He concluded that the explosion occurred close to 7:17 A.M. on June 30 and that the fireball came hurtling across the sky from south-southwest to north-northeast. As it was to be resolved later, his time was very close to the present estimate of 7:14, his June 30 date was correct, but his direction of south-southwest was not to agree with the currently accepted direction of south-southeast to north-northwest.

Voznesensky felt that the "Khatanga" (Stony Tunguska) meteorite, as he termed it, was not a single object but numerous meteorite fragments and a large parent object. The large mass, he said, probably blasted out a crater similar to the one in Arizona. He went on to draw comparisons between the American Indian legend associated with the Arizona fall as "a fiery chariot falling from the sky and penetrating the ground" and the Tungus legend citing their god of fire, Ogdy. Voznesensky's work was to help persuade the authorities back in Leningrad to finance another expedition by Kulik. Perhaps what caught their keenest attention was Voznesensky's statement that the meteorite could prove to be a very profitable object to excavate: "The search for an investigation of the Khatanga meteorite could prove a very profitable subject, particularly if this meteorite turned out to belong to the iron class," he wrote.

KULIK GETS HIS EXPEDITION

Although a number of Kulik's fellow scientists still doubted that a large meteorite had fallen, his old friend Vernadsky again was able to persuade the Expedition Research Commission of the Academy of Sciences that another expedition was in order. Accordingly, Kulik and a research assistant named Gyulikh left Leningrad on February 12, 1927. Again he crossed the desolate Siberian countryside by the Trans-Siberian Railroad, but this time he continued eastward past Kansk to Tayshet, some 900

This rare photograph of Kulik (right) and Suslov together shows them working over a magnetometer. The photograph was taken in March 1927 by Suslov's wife, Vera.

COURTESY: COMMITTEE ON METEORITES, RUSSIAN ACADEMY OF SCIENCES

kilometers nearly due south of Vanavara. Meanwhile Suslov, also convinced that a large meteorite had fallen, wrote a letter of recommendation for Kulik. It was sent to the local Soviet political official who had the authority to put Kulik in touch with the Tungus chiefs.

On March 14, after buying food and other supplies and equipment, Kulik and Gyulikh began the long trip north to Vanavara by horse-drawn sleds. This was a good time to travel overland in north-central Siberia. The ground was still frozen and lightly covered by snow, which made travel by a horse-drawn sled the swiftest way to cross the 900 kilometer distance. Had they tried to make the journey in January or February the snow would have been too deep. Even in March there could be heavy storms as the harsh Siberian winter lingered into spring, sometimes plunging the thermometer to -40 degrees Fahrenheit. In summer such travel would be difficult and slow because the ground was largely marshlands and swamp with dense singing clouds of mosquitoes.

Their route took them first northward to the Angara River, which they then followed eastward for five days until they reached Kezhma, where they took on more food and supplies. By this time they had traveled some 600 kilometers. There were no accurate maps to guide them through this wilderness, and their compasses often gave them inaccurate readings due

Once a small training post numbering a few hundred, today Vanavara supports about 10,000 inhabitants, most of them mineral exploration engineers and geologists. Newer buildings (left) stand in sharp contrast to the log cottages of 50 and more years ago (right). Boarded over sidewalks prevent walkers from sinking into the soft permafrost after the spring thaw. PHOTO BY GALLANT

to their high latitude of about 60 degrees north. On March 22 they left Kezhma and three days later reached the Vanavara trading post with its few modest houses of wooden planks and two trading depots.

When I was there in July, one of the driest summers people could remember, the Stony Tunguska River at the edge of town was gentle, and the elevated streets were firm dirt pockmarked with countless potholes. Football-size rocks which frost had poked up through the surface, and which for some reason no one bothers to remove, added to the obstacle course. There is a saying in Russia that there are no roads, only directions. Traffic consisted mostly of large trucks with rocks stuck in their tire treads, military vehicles, and motorcycles, although there were some bicycles. The windshields of virtually every truck and car were spiderwebs of glass cracked by rocks plucked from the roadway and thrown by deeply treaded tires. In more recent times the streets have been built up to a height of six feet or more above the permafrost level to avoid the muddy ground caused by the thawing during spring and summer. The side-walks along the main streets leading to the town's two restaurants, general store, bakery, and long barracks for oil exploration workers are wooden walkways that prevent those on foot from sinking into the soft permafrost come summer. Siberian huskies with their clear blue eyes roam the streets, apparently homeless, and endless numbers of Holstein cows often block traffic, lying on the wooden walkways or on the occasional patch of grass between the streets and sidewalks.

A RELUCTANT LYUCHETKAN IS WON OVER

Suslov's letter of recommendation had requested the local Soviet political official to put Kulik in touch with the Tungus Ilya Potapovich Petrov, or Lyuchetkan, whose tepee appears in an earlier chapter. There was good reason to believe that Lyuchetkan knew the location of the epicenter. But it was less certain that he would agree to guide Kulik over the frozen swamps and through the taiga wilderness to the fall site of the suspected meteorite.

The meeting between the two did not start off well. Lyuchetkan began by saying that he was very reluctant even to enter the enchanted area himself, and to guide foreigners there was unthinkable. It was, after all, a forbidden and sacred land. But Lyuchetkan's reluctance was no match for Kulik's determination. Kulik offered two sacks of flour in exchange for Lyuchetkan's services. Lyuchetkan warned that the journey would not be easy. Kulik offered his reluctant guide building materials for the roof and floor of his house. Lyuchetkan added that the taiga could be brutal. There would be many creeks and rivers to cross, gorges to scramble up, swamps and bogs to negotiate, and low mountains to climb, as well as endless swarms of mosquitoes. Kulik said there also could be several rolls of fabrics for clothing. Lyuchetkan nodded. A deal had been struck.

Before setting out, Kulik wanted to spend several days recording interviews with Tungus eyewitnesses of the explosion. Lyuchetkan said that he knew of several such people and agreed to bring Kulik to them. Some of the Tungus Kulik approached were reluctant to talk about the event. Others became angry and refused outright even to mention it. But many were willing to speak with him. Kulik was fascinated by the mystical aura that sometimes seemed to cloud descriptions. An enraged Ogdy had visited them, the Tungus maintained, and the fire god had put a curse on the epicenter region. Anyone who dared enter it surely would be cursed likewise. There even were accounts of herds of reindeer being sacrificed to appease the angry and vindictive god.

During the interviews almost all eyewitnesses mentioned the searing heat that accompanied the explosion. "The shirt

A book about the Tunguska event, Tunguska Marvel, *by V. K. Zhuravlev and F. U. Zegel, displays the frowning image of the vindictive fire god, Ogdy.*

was almost burned off my back," as S. Semenov had recounted. In all the literature Kulik had read about meteorite falls, he had never come across mention of an intense wave of heat accompanying a fall. At the time, he speculated that a meteorite the presumed size of the Tunguska object indeed might be capable of generating much heat on impact with the ground.

Twice Kulik and Lyuchetkan tried to enter the roadless taiga with horses, but twice they were forced to return because of deep snow. Kulik's diary best describes the ordeal: "The trip was based on the guide's reassuring us that we could follow a deer track. But the first dozen kilometers convinced us that the track existed only at the beginning of winter, for it was buried beneath 60 centimeters of snow. The horses would sink into the soft snow up to their breast bones. The loads of supplies and equipment were pushed this way and that and torn by the branches and rough tree bark of the taiga that crowded in from all sides. Our caravan continuously got stuck in dense thickets since the horses could not go through the forest as easily as the deer slips through lightly. After endless reloadings of sacks of fodder, and with the horses strained to the breaking point in the deep snow, we returned to the trading post to work out a different way to travel."

Finally, on April 8, Kulik, his assistant, and Lyuchetkan again loaded their packhorses with enough food to last about a month and headed westward along the Stony Tunguska River for some 35 kilometers until they reached the Chamba River. That river took them northeast for about 10 kilometers where, that night, they stopped to rest at the hut of the Tungus Pavel Aksenov (Okhchen), who agreed to join them as a second guide. This first part of the journey had been extremely difficult, Kulik later saying that he had never known such hardship. He and his assistant were both exhausted and ill from an inadequate diet, but Kulik's dogged determination drove them on. The next morning they reloaded their supplies onto pack reindeer and followed the Chamba River for another 50 kilometers before leaving the river and proceeding due north toward the edge of the region of fallen trees.

By mid-April the small party had trudged an additional 45 kilometers northward. On crossing the Makirta River, they began to enter the region of flattened forest. At this point Okhchen said he did not want to go farther, but Kulik persuaded him to continue for just a few days more. On April 15, the group reached the base of the twin-peaked mountain,

Mount Shakharma. On climbing the mountain Kulik was astonished. He could hardly believe his eyes. From horizon to horizon, across some 25 kilometers, there was utter devastation. Uncountable thousands of trees had been torn from the ground by the pressure wave. Their uprooted ends pointed to the north while their tops pointed southward. Birch, cedar, larch, and pine limbs were strewn everywhere. Not even the wildest descriptions of the Tungus could have prepared him for what lay before him, a chaos of twisted, broken, and scorched limbs that left him dumbfounded. He was speechless and simply

When Kulik first viewed this broad area of forest on April 15, 1927 he was overwhelmed by the utter devastation that lay before him from horizon to horizon. His vantage point was from Mount Shakharma on the distant horizon. Today the luxuriant forest conceals virtually all traces of the 1908 blast.

PHOTO BY GALLANT

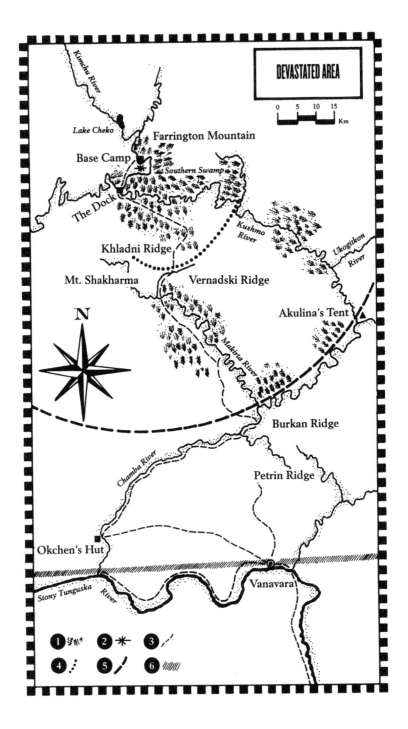

stared. Lyuchetkan and Okhchen stood beside him with fear in their eyes. Lyuchetkan slowly raised his arm, pointed over the macabre scene toward the northern horizon and said solemnly, "That is where the thunder and lightning fell down."

Later, Kulik wrote:

> A very hilly, almost mountainous, region stretches away...toward the northern horizon. In the north the distant hills along the Khushma River are covered with a white shroud of snow half a meter thick. From our observation point no sign of forest can be seen, for everything has been devastated and burned, and around the edge of this dead area the young twenty-year-old forest growth has moved forward furiously, seeking sunshine and life. One has an uncanny feeling when one sees 20- to 30-inch thick giant trees snapped across like twigs, and their tops hurled many meters away to the south. [Beyond this zone of death] is the taiga, the endless, mighty taiga, for which terrestrial fires and winds hold no terrors, for they leave no greater scars than scratches on the hands and face of one of its people.

Kulik had become the first scientific investigator to gaze on this bizarre scene. He suspected that the fall point of the meteorite lay several kilometers across the basin below him and probably just beyond the ridge of hills on the northern horizon. Sixty-five years later I stood atop that ridge of hills and gazed

---

Map shows the extent of devastation of the region between Farrington Mountain and Vanavara as observed by Krinov during the 1929-30 expedition. Symbols are as follows: 1) felled area of forest; 2) presumed impact site by Southern Swamp; 3) Kulik's route from Vanavara to the Base Camp; 4) extent of burned area; 5) extent of devastated forest; and 6) extent of explosive wave effect (AFTER KRINOV)
MAP BY RICK BRITTON

southward at Mount Shakharma as Yuriy continued to describe Kulik's hardships, hopes, disappointments, and exhilaration during the 1927 expedition.

LYUCHETKAN SAYS "NO"

"Roy, respected friend," Yuriy said to me, "can you imagine Kulik's excitement on feeling that he must be nearing his goal? And his eagerness to push on, despite his fatigue and dread of having to hack his way with axes through the chaos of fallen trees across the basin now below us? But can you also imagine his frustration when he turned to Lyuchetkan and told the Tungus to lead on through the scorched and tangled remains of the forest, only to see Lyuchetkan shake his head and frown in anger and refuse to go a step farther? Lyuchetkan would only repeat the story of his brothers, whose herds of reindeer and everything else had been incinerated by the explosion—dogs, tepee, clothing, furs, and all their stores. And he again told Kulik that the land to the north was sacred."

Kulik was reluctant to penetrate the vast region before him without Lyuchetkan. Disappointed, he returned to Vanavara; but, determined to reach his goal, he hired Russian muzhiks— peasants from the Kezhma area along the Angara River. It was then the end of April. Three days by sled brought them once again to the Chamba River, which was high with the spring melt water of snow, snarled with numerous rapids and blocks of ice. Kulik decided it would be better to build rafts and navigate first up the Chamba River toward Mount Shakharma, then along the Khushmo River, and finally into the devastated taiga. Kulik was determined to press on this time and let nothing turn him back.

After spending six days building the rafts, they set out. The river was fierce and the going difficult and dangerous. One

In June 1927, before reaching what he believed to be the epicenter region, Kulik built "The Dock," the first of his two camps. It consisted of a log cabin with a raised platform for sleeping, a shelter area with a hearth for cooking, and a storage hut. Later he added a banya, *or steam bath hut.*   PHOTO BY GALLANT

night one of the rafts broke free and sped downriver. Fortunately they found it, with all their supplies and equipment undamaged. On May 13 they reached the mouth of the Khushmo River (see map on page 56). From here they had to travel upriver, and the rafts had to be pulled by horses. Seven days later they entered the first devastated region of forest. In early June, Kulik decided to build the first of his two camps. The one on the Khushmo is called The Dock, and consisted of a log cabin with a raised platform for sleeping, a shelter area with a hearth for cooking, and a storage hut.

When Yuriy guided me and my interpreter and colleague, Kathy Rossovskaya, to this spot in early August of 1992 he pointed to where the storage hut once stood before it was destroyed by bears in search of food. The cabin, made of logs 8 to 10 inches in diameter, looked as sound as the day it was built. When Yuriy, Kathy, and I arrived at the camp and slipped out of our backpacks, we were greeted by a grinning and amiable hunter named Vitaliy Voronov. He was dressed in khaki trousers, sneakers, and a tan shirt with sleeves rolled up, and wore a red bandanna. Hanging from a rawhide thong looped around his neck, and secured by a second thong tied around his waist, was a heavy bark sheath containing one of the largest hunting knives I have ever seen. A high-powered army rifle, loaded, leaned against the shelter wall. Hanging from a tripod of poles safely out of burning range of a vigorous fire was a bucket of boiling water. After introductions and greetings, a young man of 16 or 17, who was Vitaliy's apprentice being taught to hunt and guide, produced a spit of five huge trout which he had caught an hour earlier in the river only a few yards away. One by one the fish were slipped into the boiling water head first and allowed to cook for about three minutes. The rest is very memorable history.

That night as we sat around the campfire, Vitaliy, while whittling the bark off a long, thin sapling, told Tungus stories that have been handed down over many generations. As a young man he lived with a Tungus family and had learned their ways. At one stage, he lived alone in the taiga for three years, living off the land. According to one account, when he returned to Vanavara it took several months for him to adjust to having other people around. Unused to furniture, he would squat in a corner in silence for hours at a time, longing for the aroma and sounds of his beloved taiga. Today his reputation as a hunter and a person who is at one with the taiga spans the breadth of

The vindictive fire god Ogdy lives on in this tree portrait carved by an unknown member of an earlier expedition. Kathy looks on.   PHOTO BY RITA KRUMIN

Russia, and his knowledge of the ways of the Tungus is surpassed by few. Yuriy had arranged for Vitaliy to meet us at The Dock so that I might interview him about the vanishing culture of the Tungus.

WHO ARE THE TUNGUS?

"The early Tungus settlers came to the Angara River more than three hundred years ago," he began, as Kathy translated. "Their first big settlement was Kezhma. My Russian ancestors came to live in Kezhma among the Tungus. These nomadic people did not trust the Russians, who were eager to trade for sable and other furs. According to legend, the fur trade with the Tungus

The woman with Vitaliy Baronov is one of the few surviving pure Tungus. As a child she was part of a nomad tribe, traveling with her clan's herd of reindeer as the men hunted for food and trapped sable and other fur-bearing animals to barter with Russian traders. Vitaliy, about five feet seven inches tall, is a famed hunter who lived with Tungus tribespeople for several years when he was a child and a young man. PHOTO BY GALLANT

began when the Russians captured a Tungus boy, taught him Russian and learned the Tungus language from him. They then freed him on condition that he show them the nomad trails. And that is how the first trading began.

"The Tungus would bring their reindeer caravans heavy with furs to the Angara River. Eventually the Russians entered the taiga as far as the Stony Tunguska River and established a number of trading posts, including the one at Vanavara, which was then called Anavar, meaning "a place lucky for hunting." In older days Anavar was a large nomad camp where the various Tungus tribes would meet. That is why the Russians decided to build a merchants' lodge there. The first houses in Vanavara were a dance house, a small chapel where the Tungus were baptized, and the lodge, called *pokruta*, where the trading took place.

"My parents moved to Vanavara in 1932 and I was born there ten years later. My first memories of the Tungus people date from the time I was about five. There were many of them here then, but no more. When we lived on the Chamba I was accepted in all tepees. I played with, and grew up with, Tungus children. I went on their nomad treks for 200, 300, 500 kilometers through the taiga. They knew perfectly well how to reach their destination. Since I was only a child, I was not permitted to speak, except at certain times, only to observe and learn. They taught me how to reach any place, any area with deer, bears, sables. Their nomad trails were the trails of the wild animals. Wherever the trails crossed, the clans would meet from time to time, exchange news, and talk about hunting.

"Under communism, the Tungus hunters could no longer hunt and trade independently. There was a big collective farm run by the government, the *kolkhoz*, which they all had to belong to. No one had his own reindeer herds any more. There was only one big herd, and that was owned by the state. The hunters were supposed to sell their furs only to the state at a fixed price. All the Tungus children were sent away to attend boarding schools far from home. And that is when the most terrible mistake was made. Children were taken away from their natural environment, uprooted from their culture, from their parents, from the Tungus way of life. A thin thread of inherited traditions and culture was broken. By the time the children finished school away from home, they had forgotten their people's history. These youngsters no longer wanted to return to a life in the taiga. That meant an abrupt decline of reindeer breeding. But something even worse was happening.

"The Tungus mainly traded their furs in exchange for alcohol. Few of them dealt with money until about the 1960s. And because of heavy drinking among the hunters the death rate became high and life expectancy low. A strange thing began to occur—the Tungus stopped producing pure Tungus families. The women preferred to marry anyone but their drunken reindeer herders.

"The personality and the moral character of the men were decaying. They were no longer real hunters and stopped being the leaders of their families, of their clans. All of this happened gradually, not suddenly. I can remember that there were still reindeer caravans as late as the 1950s. And I have vivid memories of the old, real Tungus hunters and reindeer breeders. On the Chamba River there lived the Tungus clans of the Pickunovs, the Aksyonovs. Yes, there were still strong family groups then. But Russian names soon were given to the infants when they were baptized. Earlier, the Tungus had named their children after objects and living things in their environment— Axe, Knife, Fox, River, and so on. But then they were given mainly biblical names: Avel, Naum, Afanasiy, Andrey for the boys. The girls were named Mariya, Darya, Anna, Polina. So in a short time the Tungus lost even their names, and the state forbade them to practice their pagan religion. Ogdy was dead.

"Only the Evenki living in the area of the three Tungus rivers—the Podkamennaya Tunguska River, the Angara River, and the Nizhnyaya Tunguska River—are the ones called the Tungus people. When my parents came to Vanavara in the early 1930s there were several thousand of them. Today there probably are fewer than 50 pure Tungus, and maybe another 150 mixed Tungus. Those numbers include all the Tungus not only in Vanavara but in other trading posts of the entire administrative district, five trading posts in all. At most you will find ten Tungus in this or that trading post, but in some none at all. There probably are only about 50 reindeer left in the trading post of Mutarai, the same in Strelka. The reindeer began to die out when the Evenki started to cut off the antlers of young Siberian stags to sell to the Japanese. Deprive the animals of their antlers and the herd is weakened. Breeding reindeer without their antlers will not produce a healthy generation. The animals become smaller and subject to diseases. So over the past twenty-five years or so we sadly have witnessed the slow death of an entire, once proud and thriving, culture."

THE SHAMAN'S TALE

Sixty-five years earlier, as Kulik and his assistant sat around their evening campfire at the very spot where Vitaliy later related to me his experiences with the Tungus, Kulik's guides undoubtedly spoke of happier and healthier times for their people. As sparks from the fire streaked skyward and seemed to mix with the diamond-bright stars, perhaps they even told a shaman story similar to this one recalled by Vitaliy, recounting an event that occurred during his nomad life when a boy.

"The most horrible thing that could happen during a hunt was the loss of the dogs," Vitaliy began. "If you lose the dogs, the hunt is over. During one hunt I was on with my Tungus family, the dogs ran ahead through the snow to chase an elk. When they did not come back we returned to our tepee and waited. We waited one day, then another, then the third day. Our nomad camp was in mourning. When the dogs are absent for one day, there is always hope that they will return. If they are not back in two days, we become alarmed. And when they do not return after three days, they usually are dead.

"By the end of the third day we had lost all hope. No one spoke in the tepee except the old man. We, the young hunters, had no right to talk. I remember the night vividly. It was late. The wind was so strong that the whole taiga was moaning. No one went to sleep. Then the old woman, whose name was Nadyora, meaning "hope," began to cook food for the dogs. She took a piece of birch bark and with a knife like the one I wear cut out of the bark the shapes of three running dogs. She then bound them with a thin string of rawhide and poised them above the dish of hot food, their heads pointed down as if eating hungrily. She next took the bowl outside and walked a short way into the taiga. And I heard the wind howling and the woman singing. She hit a stick against the bowl. Bang! Bang! Bang! and continued to sing, but I could not hear the words clearly, only that she sang about the dogs. Then she returned to the tepee and placed the bowl just outside the entrance. After that she took her sleeping position with her head pointed at the entrance, as is the custom of the hostess who must always be alert. Everyone went to sleep after that.

"In the morning I was the first to awake and quietly went outside. All the dogs were lying near the entrance of the tepee and the bowl was empty. Twice I was the witness of such a shaman method of making the dogs return safely."

CHAPTER SEVEN

KULIK FINDS
the EPICENTER

*T*he next morning I was awakened by the crackling of a fire outside my Tungus tepee. Kathy was feeding small sticks to the flames and boiling water for tea. After a breakfast of dark Russian bread and hot instant cereal, we walked over to the edge of a steep gravel embankment that led down to the Khushmo River. As I was then looking down on a nearby bend in that river, years earlier Kulik from his raft had looked up to the place where I stood, his bespectacled eyes searching for a suitable place to build his first camp.

My image of Kulik on his raft was suddenly replaced by a grinning Vitaliy standing while poling his way around the bend toward us in a small flat-bottom boat shaped something like a canoe. He had been fishing. Made of planking, and a little more than four meters long, the boat had one seat spanning the mid-section. A bottom of sheet metal revealed telltale patches of tar used to seal leaks. Over a period of four and a half days, Vitaliy had poled his way from Vanavara, along the Stony Tunguska, up the Chamba, and then up the Khushmo to meet us at The Dock. In a few days he and the boy would return to

This Tungus tepee made by Vitaliy was to be my temporary home some 50 meters from The Dock. Vitaliy tends the fire while his assistant and Kathy look on.

Vanavara, covering the 70-kilometer distance in about five days, along the way being scrutinized by curious bears.

IN KULIK'S WAKE

Vitaliy is as keenly interested in the Kulik expeditions, and in protecting the Tungus region from damage done by oil exploration, as are Academician Vasiliev and Yuriy. Since our meeting in 1992 Vitaliy has been put in a position of authority to monitor those wanting to gain access to the epicenter region. As he maneuvered the small boat against the riverbank that morning, he waved me down, saying that he wanted to spend part of the day poling me along the Khushmo to retrace part of Kulik's trip along this river.

I can recall few times in my life when I have felt more at ease and more a part of the land than during those tranquil and unhurried hours on the river with *Boyo* ("friend") Vitaliy. Although we spoke infrequently, we somehow sensed the thoughts of each other—namely, respect and love for this wilderness. I found myself feeling as at home in Vitaliy's taiga as I do in my own Maine north woods. And I'm sure that he would feel as at home in my woods as he does in his beloved taiga.

Because of the dryness and lateness of the summer season, the river was low and calm. Several times I had to climb out to

Boyo Vitaliy poles us along the Khushmo River, calm and serene in its summer mood. When Kulik moved his supply boats along this river during the spring ice breakup, he was hurled into the icy water, nearly drowned and crushed by the ice (see p. 85). PHOTO BY ROSSOVSKAYA

cross a gravel bar by foot while Vitaliy waded and pulled the boat over the stream bed's glistening pebbles. Bird song filled the air, beaver swam unconcerned in front of us, a startled duck beat its wings and ran along the water as it took flight, and trout seemingly the size of dolphins jumped for low-flying insects. Twice we stopped by deep shaded pools where Vitaliy expertly worked his fishing pole whittled the night before while telling us Tungus tales. The first strike came after thirty seconds, the second in another forty seconds. Both were fat trout more than a foot long. Deftly he smacked the head of each fish on a rock and tossed them into the boat. Within the next five minutes he caught an equal number of trout. There would be fish for dinner, and breakfast tomorrow.

Guide Vitaliy (left, Kathy at right) dug this 10,000-year-old mammoth tusk out of the loose sediments of the Khushmo River banks, a fossil hunter's paradise. A few years later he recovered the lower jaw of a saber-toothed tiger. Vitaliy's river trip in his small boat from Vanavara to The Dock took four and a half days.

PHOTO BY GALLANT

An occasional large cedar slumped like a frontier gate across a narrow part of the river would force us to bend low as a strong thrust of Vitaliy's pole glided us beneath it. On his raft, Kulik had encountered many such fallen trees blocking his way and had to chop his way through with axes. Our boat scraped its way through small forests of lily pads. Even in the deeper sections of the river the water was so clear that it seemed not to be there at all. Fish in deep pools appeared to be suspended motionless in the air. Along one high sloping bank the soil, gravel, and clay sediments were layered like a giant lasagna—a fossil hunter's paradise. Several years earlier Vitaliy had seen a suspicious-looking object sticking out of those sediments. He stopped and dug out a seventy-pound mammoth tusk as smooth and polished as if it still belonged to its owner. During another trip he came home with the lower jawbone of a saber-toothed tiger. There are Tungus accounts of the late spring thawing and slumping of the soft riverbanks revealing entire carcasses of mammoths who roamed these forests 10,000 years ago. The cold and deeply frozen ground—in winter as hard as a concrete tennis court—that preserved Vitaliy's mammoth tusk and saber-toothed jawbone also has been responsible for preserving the peat and trees felled by the 1908 blast. The scars of catastrophe do not heal quickly in the land of eternal frost.

How the peace and calm of my hours along the Khushmo contrasted with Kulik's ordeal during his 1927 expedition! The swollen river was then a raging torrent with rapids and deep water from the spring melt and runoff. Instead of ducks and beaver for companions, Kulik and his small party had boulders of ice the size of mammoth heads crashing against their rafts. After building The Dock, Kulik's immediate quest was to concentrate his ebbing energy and failing health on locating the fall point of the meteorite and its presumed giant crater.

THE CHURGIM CREEK AND MOUNT CASCADE

The following morning after our breakfast of trout, Yuriy, Kathy, and I climbed into our heavy backpacks and, after saying our farewells to Vitaliy and the boy, set out northward through the taiga. Every once in awhile Yuriy would let out a short series of yelps intended to alert the bears and the region's very large wolves to our presence. My hopes were that they would be frightened away rather than attracted. After about an hour I began to hear the sound of falling water. We were approaching the Churgim Creek and its 15-meter-high waterfall. When we reached it we were standing at the base of a steeply sloping cliff face of sharply angled rock. Mist from the waterfall felt cool and refreshing against my face. Judging from the height of the canyon walls through which the Churgim Creek flows and continues its long erosional process, the waterway is very old geologically.

After carefully picking our way among the recesses and outcroppings of the rock face to the waterfall's top, we slipped out of our packs and stretched out to rest at the base of a 300-meter-high hill called Mount Cascade. Squatting beside me and pointing with a long strand of grass, Yuriy said that this probably was where the Tungus herdsman Vasiliy Dzhenkoul's nomad camp had been located on that morning of June 30 in 1908. And pointing up the canyon northward, he said that the fire came roaring through where we were now resting and incinerated between 600 and 700 of Dzhenkoul's reindeer, his dogs, and all his stores and tepees. Yuriy then related the following account of how Kulik was first led to this spot.

"The Tungus and Russian traders in the Vanavara region all came to know Kulik as a famous man, a scientist, and called him Professor. He also had the reputation for his ability to treat people with illness. His father was a highly respected doctor and most likely taught his son a number of useful remedies for

The firestorm of the 1908 blast came roaring out of Southern Swamp and through the canyon formed by Churgim Creek, which drains the great swamp. After scaling the 15-meter-high rock face of the water falls, Yuriy, Kathy, and I rested at a spot near where the Tungus herdsmen Dzhenkoul's tepee, stores, and herd of about 700 reindeer were incinerated.   PHOTO BY GALLANT

various medical problems. Once, when Kulik was at the Chamba River, a Tungus shaman named Vasiliy approached him and asked Kulik to cure his daughter, who was seriously ill.

It turned out that her condition was too advanced, and the girl died. She was buried near their nomadic camp and, according to Tungus tradition, the shaman's clan left that camp and migrated to a different one.

"In appreciation for Kulik's attention, shaman Vasiliy offered to show him the most direct route to the "enchanted" region, or epicenter of the explosion. He arrived in his best shaman garments and led Kulik here, to this very location on the Churgim Creek. He then pointed and said, '*Boyo*, you must go along the fire rivulet [along the rock canyon leading to the Southern Swamp].' The shaman then left. And that is how Kulik successfully reached his destination. But there is more to

Sand Dune Hill as photographed by Suslov in October 1928 (left) and by the author in August 1992 (right). Eighty-four years after the 1908 explosion the radial pattern and alignment of felled trees are still evident.
LEFT: COURTESY: COMMITTEE ON METEORITES, RUSSIAN ACADEMY OF SCIENCES;
RIGHT: PHOTO BY GALLANT

the story. Later, Kulik learned that shaman Vasiliy was killed by his own people, evidently because he violated the taboo of revealing the location of the enchanted land."

This was not to be the last incident of a person being killed, or disappearing in connection with the Tunguska event.

After telling the story of shaman Vasiliy, Yuriy walked over to an uprooted tree about two feet in diameter. It had been bleached over the decades by the summer Sun and polished smooth by the erosion of frost and melting snow. The exposed roots were pointed northward. From the roots to a distance of about a meter along the stem was a deeply-scarred V-shaped burn mark left by Ogdy's firewind.

Leaving our packs temporarily, we climbed to the top of Mount Cascade. The spectacular view made me gasp. Far across the luxuriant forest basin to the south were the twin peaks of Mount Shakharma, where Lyuchetkan had given Kulik his sweeping view of the devastation and beyond which the Tungus had refused to go. To the north was a vast and sprawling flat region, the Southern Swamp. When Kulik had viewed the terrain from this very spot, he had had few doubts that he had found the epicenter region, or fall point of the meteorite. From here the devastation appeared even greater than what he had seen from the top of Mount Shakharma, for now he could see beyond Mount Cascade and the Churgim Heights. Although much more extensive, the destruction was the same as before—a twisted and tangled mass of broken limbs and uprooted trees strangely aligned.

BURN SCARS AND THE "TELEGRAPH-POLE FOREST"

Before descending the mountain and continuing our hike to Kulik's main camp, we picked our way through the surrounding forest on the north-facing slope. Although forest growth had been rapid over the years, I saw hundreds of relics of scorched and felled trees, many snapped off at midstem height. I also saw numerous examples of still-standing trees which at first mystified Kulik and came to be called "telegraph poles."

From The Dock, as his headquarters, Kulik concentrated his interest in the broad flat region of the Southern Swamp, which he believed was the fall point of the meteorite, and the central point from which the felled trees were tumbled outward in a radial pattern. To test his suspicion, Kulik made several daily excursions, as described in a booklet he wrote and entitled *In Search of the Tunguska Wonder:*

This 1928 photograph taken by Suslov shows the "telegraph pole" forest. Those trees directly beneath the point of explosion were stripped of most of their branches due to the downward pressure wave. The bark was seared away by the following firewind.

COURTESY: COMMITTEE ON METEORITES, RUSSIAN ACADEMY OF SCIENCES

I made my second camp at the top of the pass and began a circuit of the mountains rimming the Great Cauldron [of which the Southern Swamp is a part]; first I went westward for dozens of kilometers over the naked hill crests; here the felled trees all lay with their tops pointing west. Leaving the mountains to the south of me, I completed a huge circle around the whole cauldron. As if bewitched, the felled trees lay with their tops now pointed north. I returned to camp and again set out, this time eastward crossing many of the bald patches of forested hills, and the tree-tops here also pointed east. By now exhausted, I strained every muscle and nerve and once again headed south almost to the Khushmo. The tops of the felled trees also pointed southward. I had no doubts: I had circled the center of the fall! With a fiery stream of hot gases and cold solid bodies the meteorite had struck the cauldron, with its hills, tundra, and swamp. The stream of hot gases with the swarm of bodies struck and penetrated the ground in the same manner as a stream of water that strikes a flat surface, the liquid splashing outward in all four directions. And so it was the combination of both a direct impact and explosive recoil that this powerful picture of destruction was created. But according to the laws of physics, there should also be a place where the forest remained standing [like telegraph poles], losing their bark, leaves and branches from the heat.

Kulik later found those standing trees stripped of their branches and described them as "dead forests enchanted as if in a fairy tale."

Krinov, who was to join Kulik on his 1930 expedition, also mentions the central telegraph-pole forest of dead trees, plus clusters of more such trees in certain depressed, protected areas. The trees remained standing, stripped of most of their limbs and with their tops broken off. In his diary, Kulik described working his way through his old, dead forest on mornings when the wind rose and having to be constantly on guard against the twenty-year-old giants toppling around him. "As we went along we kept our eyes on the treetops so that, if they fell, we should have time to jump aside. This method of advance had its unpleasant side, for with our eyes turned upwards we did not see what was under our feet, and we continually stumbled against adders [poisonous snakes] that abound everywhere in this region."

When I walked among many of the telegraph poles still standing in 1992, and across many kilometers of taiga, I asked Yuriy if there were venomous snakes in the forest. He shook his head, but I couldn't tell if he was shaking it yes or no. In any event, perhaps because my eyes were often skyward, I failed to see a single snake.

A DIET OF *PUCHKI* AND, MAYBE, THE HORSE?

The area of the epicenter of the explosion included, in addition to the Southern Swamp, hills, ridges, isolated summits, and flat tundra, marsh, lakes, and streams. Everywhere within the "cauldron" and on surrounding hillsides for several kilometers around, Kulik found clear evidence of "uniformly continuous scorching." He also examined a number of structures that led him to think that the parent meteorite probably had fragmented and thrown off a number of smaller meteorites. He describes these features in *In Search of the Tunguska Wonder*:

> Finally, in the northeast section of the cauldron I discovered dozens of flat craters, like lunar craters. They were most noticeable in the tundra that had been burnt and had not yet recovered its vegetation. The craters varied in diameter, most being typically from ten to fifty meters. Their depth seldom exceeded about four meters, and their floors were covered with marsh moss. I cannot say how deeply the meteorites had penetrated into the tundra and rocks, since I was unable to walk around the whole area flattened by them; nor could I start digging because we had food left for only three or

four days. Our road back was a long one, and our one thought now was to return safely. It would be a retreat in the full sense of the word.

Their journey back to Vanavara proved to be just as difficult as Kulik had feared. Their food supply was almost gone because they had not been able to shoot elk and other game they had counted on finding. They managed to shoot four ducks about the time they shook out the last flour sack, and they caught a few fish. For the nine days of their trip they lived mostly on "leftovers of cheerfulness" and the edible peeled roots and stem of a plant Kulik called *puchki*. A number of times, Kulik wrote in his diary, "we tenderly evaluated the weight of our last [food] reserve—our exhausted four-legged friend, the horse."

By the time Kulik's party returned to Vanavara in late June his reputation in the region had been well established—the outsider who dared to defy the taboo and enter the enchanted land of the Tungus, without coming to any harm. However, according to Yuriy, soon after their return to the trading post one of Kulik's expedition workers disappeared under mysterious circumstances and was later found dead. Like shaman Vasiliy's death—the mystery of the worker's death was never solved.

Kulik was convinced that he had located the fall point of the main meteorite body and many of the craters formed by an accompanying swarm of smaller meteorites, each of which he estimated at 130 tons. "How deeply those smaller bodies penetrated the ground is impossible to say," Kulik wrote, "because we have no knowledge of similar events in history. World literature has not preserved a single historical event similar to this one, a case history that could provide us a key to a reasonable explanation."

In December 1927 he presented his August 19 report for the Krasnoyarsk authorities to the Regional Executive

Committee of the Academy of Sciences. The committee promised full support for future expeditions. Part of the report said that "the results of even a cursory examination exceeded all the tales of the eyewitnesses and my wildest expectations.... [And] the positive results of my expedition are irrefutable. Their unique scientific significance, like the significance of the Tunguska fall itself, will be fully appreciated only in history and it is necessary to record all the remaining traces of this fall for posterity."

He then eagerly began to sketch out plans for an expedition the following year.

CHAPTER EIGHT

The EXPEDITIONS of
1928 and 1929–1930

*K*ulik's detailed notes, many interviews with Tungus tribesmen, and photographs swept away all doubts that the
1908 event was simply an earthquake in some remote region of
Siberia. The magazine, newspaper, and technical articles he
wrote about his 1927 investigation quickly gained worldwide
attention and put Kulik in the scientific spotlight.

A Moscow newspaper said of the event: "In a densely pop-
ulated region a similar phenomenon would be one of the most
appalling catastrophes in human history." An astronomer in the
United States wrote that the event was "the most astonishing
phenomenon of its kind in scientific annals." And an authority
on meteorites at the Colorado Museum of Natural History
urged an American expedition to the site of the explosion "to
secure what is yet available of the greatest message from the
depths of space that has ever reached our planet."

Almost overnight Kulik had awakened deep concern in
people of all walks of life, and he basked in the glow of his
international prestige. But despite his reputation as a skilled
researcher, Kulik was not without critics, those who were skep-
tical about his claim that a giant meteorite was the 1908

culprit. The well-known meteorologist Mul'tanovsky suggested that maybe there simply had been a huge wind storm accompanied by a fire. While Kulik never doubted that a meteorite had caused the destruction, he sometimes puzzled over the ability of a meteorite to cause the *kind* of widespread destruction he had observed.

THE 1928 EXPEDITION

Early in 1928, Kulik's old friend Vernadsky called a meeting of the Academy and recommended that new expeditions be organized. Accordingly, Kulik drew up plans for a two-stage investigation. The first, to depart in 1928, was to set the stage for a full-fledged expedition to last eighteen months during 1929 and 1930. The major effort would be a search of the Southern Swamp and Kulik's numerous "craters." If iron meteorite bodies were buried in the region, a combination of drilling and magnetic surveys should reveal them. Kulik also had stressed the importance of an aerial photographic survey of the entire region.

In early April, Kulik and his new assistant, Sytin, left Leningrad for Moscow where they boarded the Trans-Siberian Express for Siberia. They were later to be joined by the documentary motion picture photographer N. Strukov, who was to capture on film some remarkable episodes. Among them was Kulik's mishap on the Chamba River when he nearly drowned. By April 18 they had reached Kezhma where they hired workers to cut trails through the chaotic forest in preparation for the following year's major expedition.

One day while in Kezhma, Kulik was approached by men identifying themselves as "local officials" who said that escaped criminals were in the area. Knowing of the "rich" scientist's presence nearby, the criminals most likely would follow Kulik

This frame from the documentary movie made by filmmaker N. Strukov shows Kulik in the icy Khushmo River, when he was thrown in the water while trying to maneuver his supply boats.
COURTESY: THE COMMITTEE ON METEORITES, RUSSIAN ACADEMY OF SCIENCES

into the wilderness and then kill him, Kulik was told. From that moment on he and Sytin were nervously on their guard and seldom were more than a few feet from their guns.

By late April the group had reached Vanavara and met Strukov. But it wasn't until May 21, when the river ice began to break up, that the party of eight was able to navigate down the Stony Tunguska River with their three horses and dogs. At one stage on the raging Chamba River they had to unload the boats and hand carry supplies and equipment across the rapids to the opposite bank. Kulik took charge of pulling the empty boats across. After successfully managing the first boat, the second one was suddenly swung around by the current and overturned, sending Kulik flying. Luckily his leg was caught up in a mooring line, and he was able to pull himself to safety. He had narrowly missed a combination of drowning and being dashed against menacing rocks. Throughout it all, Strukov calmly stood by and filmed the entire episode, including a dripping and choking Kulik stumbling ashore with his eyeglasses still in place.

On June 6, after having covered more than 250 kilometers, the group arrived at The Dock on the Khushmo River. Immediately the workmen built a food storage hut perched high on stilts for protection against bears and wolves, the region's "rightful owners," as Academician Vasiliev warned us during our 1992 expedition. They also built a *banya*, a small Russian bathing hut similar to a sauna. When I visited The Dock, I cooked myself in Kulik's banya, steaming myself thoroughly by splashing small bursts of water onto a pile of rocks heated by a wood fire. The finale was a hasty dash across the few yards to the Khushmo River and a plunge into the cold water, Russian style.

Kulik's workers next cut a trail through the fallen trees over a distance of about 7 kilometers along the old Churgim streambed which drained the Southern Swamp. On arriving at the edge of the swamp, they built a lodge and an elevated storage hut at the base of Mount Stoikovich, which became the first two buildings of Kulik's Base Camp complex and served as our headquarters in 1992. Kulik then set about his topographical survey by measuring the heights of the surrounding hills. The region had never been mapped. He also surveyed an area of 100 square kilometers in preparation for magnetic surveys and drove 160 wooden stakes into "crater" locations to mark possible drilling and magnetic test sites.

Food storage huts were built by Kulik at The Dock and at his base camp. Their purpose was to protect food and other supplies from marauding bears. Despite the huts' rugged construction, bears often managed to climb up the posts and claw their way through the door to feast on sugar, dried meats, and anything else they considered edible.   PHOTO BY GALLANT

KULIK LOSES HIS CREW

Strukov, accompanied by three of the workmen, returned to Vanavara on July 14, leaving Kulik, Sytin, and two workers at the Base Camp. Kulik and Sytin continued the survey, ever on guard and not to be done in by the escaped convicts. They also collected several hundred specimens of peat and other plant matter for microscopic examination back in Leningrad. By the end of July, all four men were showing signs of vitamin deficiency because of a lack of fresh vegetables. Both workmen had become ill, one seriously so. Always concerned for the well-being of his workers, Kulik decided to send both of them back to Vanavara. Sytin was to return to Leningrad to report the expedition's difficulties to the Academy, including the lack of funds to hire new workmen to haul out the collected scientific materials for shipment to Leningrad.

On August 2, Kulik led Sytin and the two ill workmen back to Vanavara. It was about this time when he learned that the alarm about the escaped convicts was false and that the Kezhma "officials" actually were Russian merchants who illegally had been buying furs from the Tungus in exchange for homemade vodka. After learning about the merchants' activity, real village officials of Kezhma located their houses at the mouth of the Chamba River and burned them to the ground.

According to Yuriy, Kulik cunningly used this episode to further strengthen his good standing with high Soviet officials in Krasnoyarsk who could approve or deny permission to those who wanted to enter the Tungus region. He reportedly wrote to the officials and falsely accused certain individuals, by name, of being "Tungusniks," meaning those who trade with the Tungus illegally.

I asked Yuriy why he thought Kulik would engage in such deception and put other people's lives at risk. "Kulik was only human," he told me. "You must remember that the Soviet authorities under Stalin were ruthless. Anyone could be convicted without any reason and without a trial. The police could come at night and take you away, and you would never be heard of again. Or you could be arrested for simply disagreeing with an official and sent to a Gulag prison labor camp for fifteen years. Or you simply could be prohibited from ever entering a certain region again. My own opinion is that Kulik wanted to win the favor of those high Soviet officials so that in the future they would admit him into the Tungus region without problems. And it was a way to win favor by showing support of the Soviet government. It was like emergency money in the bank. This incident has never been published before, and even today it probably would not be published in Russia because no one would want to blemish the ideal image of Kulik, who was a national hero. Again, Kulik was only human and, like the rest of us, he sometimes made mistakes."

Before leaving Vanavara, with the last of his funds Kulik hired one new workman to return with him to the Base Camp. But during the journey the workman became seriously ill and was of little use to Kulik until he recovered in September. Late in October, Sytin, concerned about Kulik's health, returned with a small rescue expedition including members of the press and Suslov, who had been the first to record extensive eyewitness accounts of the explosion. Although grateful for the new arrivals, Kulik was not a man to waste time or energy. He quickly put them to work helping with magnetic measurements at various locations, including staked positions in the "crater" which today bears Suslov's name.

NEGATIVE RESULTS AND THE RETURN HOME

All the magnetic probes were negative. Although Kulik did not realize it at the time, the outdated magnetometers were of such low sensitivity that they were virtually useless for his purposes. Furthermore, if some of the tests had turned out positive, the encouraging results could have been caused not by iron meteorites but by the magnetic property of certain rock outcrops in the area. According to Krinov, who was to join the major expedition the following year, "None of Kulik's work on magnetic measurement could, therefore, be considered of serious scientific significance."

The expedition packed up and left the Base Camp on October 27, and Kulik was back in Leningrad by the end of November. Due to a bureaucratic muddle, the aerial survey had to be postponed. Although Kulik remained convinced that a huge meteorite, along with its many fragments, lay alluringly buried in the region of the Southern Swamp, he realized that the 1928 expedition had returned home empty-handed. There was not one shred of hard evidence to support his meteorite theory. But he also knew that over those six months he had fulfilled his primary goal of preparing for the upcoming major expedition. They had cleared a 7-kilometer-long trail linking The Dock with the Base Camp, had carried out extensive land surveys, constructed new buildings, excavated two "craters," and cut a drainage trench in a third. The trench had allowed them to compare soil layers of the trench wall with soil layers of the crater. A difference in the two soil profiles would help identify the 220 square-meter oval depression as a true crater. There turned out to be no difference in the soil profiles.

Increasingly, skeptics among Kulik's earth science colleagues continued to voice doubts about a meteoritic origin of the 1908 blast. Glaciologists and specialists in tundra land formations felt that Kulik's so-called "craters" most likely were natural formations in the permafrost.

THE THIRD EXPEDITION—1929–1930

Despite the skeptics, Kulik's reputation and bulldog will to continue the search won the Academy of Science's continued support for funding expeditions. So on February 24, 1929 the largest expedition yet left Leningrad. There was Kulik, assisted by Deputy Director Krinov. And there were a swamp expert, a technician to supervise drilling operations, and three enthusiastic amateurs. Along the way three others joined the expedition. About fifty horses pulled an equal number of sleds loaded with five tons of supplies and equipment. There was a drilling apparatus, hand bores, pumps for draining water, steel cable, spades, pickaxes, saws, meteorological instruments, a surveying instrument, and cameras.

When the expedition arrived at the Base Camp one of its first tasks was to dig a well, the same well that our 1992 expedition used. The water was yellow, had an unpleasant odor, and tasted awful, even after boiling. The only clean water was from The Dock on the Khushmo 7 kilometers away. How many times I recalled the invigorating plunge into the Khushmo after my *banya*, at the same time drinking my fill of that crystal clear river water!

DIGGING INTO THE SUSLOV CRATER

Kulik's first major task was a thorough investigation of the Suslov crater, which was about 30 meters across and which was located only a couple of hundred meters from the Base Camp. Kulik hoped to excavate a meteorite from it. But first the crater had to be drained by cutting a sloping trench 38 meters long, 1.5 meters wide, and 4 meters deep at its lowest point. The trench was completed on May 25, and as water came pouring out of the crater the still-frozen sphagnum moss surface gradually sank and settled onto the muddy bottom. According to Krinov, as the sphagnum settled, "it was quite possible to take it for a meteorite hole or crater." By June 27 the workers had managed to strip away the melting sphagnum while using hand

One of the small, neat oval bogs that Kulik erroneously presumed to be secondary craters of the fragmented meteorite. This one was named after the ethnographer Suslov.   PHOTO BY GALLANT

pumps to keep the crater from flooding. Then came a disappointing discovery, as described by Krinov:

"When the hole had been cleared of moss, a tree stump broken off right at the roots was discovered not far from its center. This completely unexpected find disproved conclusively the meteorite theory of the origin of the Suslov hole. Indeed, it was impossible to imagine that a tree stump could have been preserved in its natural position so near the center of a hole formed by the fall of a meteorite."

Nevertheless, Kulik insisted that excavation of the crater

continue. Meanwhile, three expedition members became ill from exhaustion caused by the hard physical labor and had to leave. Then another of the workmen came down with acute appendicitis and for several days lay unconscious and delirious. On July 3, Kulik and two others carried the stricken worker to Vanavara. After studying certain peat bogs and swamps near Vanavara, the three returned to the Base Camp on August 19. At one stage, Kulik's hopes soared when a worker found a piece of fused glass near the northern edge of the Suslov crater. On examining it, Kulik concluded that it was rock fused into glass by the impact of the meteorite, and he said as much in several articles he wrote later. But this bit of "evidence" also turned out to be misleading. Further study revealed the glass as a piece of ordinary bottle glass melted when one of the buildings caught fire on the first night of the expedition's arrival at the Base Camp on April 6. A small storage room had contained a number of objects including pieces of a broken bottle. Workers had swept up the rubbish, including the melted and rehardened glass, and dumped it in a peat bog near the edge of the Suslov crater.

Stubbornly convinced that a meteorite nevertheless rested at the bottom of the Suslov crater, Kulik set up a drilling rig at the northern edge of the hole. Drilling continued at a painfully slow pace due to the presence of heavy rock. Whenever the drill hit rock, it would have to be withdrawn and a chisel lowered into the hole and hammered to break through the rock before drilling could continue. By October, the drill had cut its way to a depth of 25 meters. Still no meteorite.

By mid-November the rivers had frozen solid and snow covered the land. Temperatures often plunged to -40 degrees Fahrenheit. On November 18, Krinov and one worker set out with a sick horse pulling a sledge loaded with peat samples and other scientific collections to be sent to laboratories in Leningrad. By the time they covered 200 kilometers, nearly all of it walking behind the sledge through deep drifts of snow, they were exhausted and their feet were frostbitten. It was essential to reach Kezhma for medical treatment, which they managed to do on November 22. Supplies were then sent to Kulik at the Base Camp. The workers who brought them reported back to Krinov that Kulik was still drilling into the Suslov crater, and they brought a written report to be telegraphed immediately to Leningrad. In it Kulik described the impossibly harsh winter conditions and begged for additional funds to pay expedition debts for supplies purchased in Vanavara. The money was telegraphed from Leningrad and arrived in January. The Academy's instructions to Kulik were to finish his work as soon as he could and return home. Krinov hired three new workers and, with a sledge loaded with fresh provisions, sent them to the Base Camp, where they arrived on January 10. Kulik was still drilling.

Hospitalized in Kezhma, Krinov had to have one of his big toes amputated to prevent gangrene from spreading. By mid-February he was released and he hired five sledges and two carriers to bring additional fresh provisions to Kulik. The worker who had accompanied Krinov from the Base Camp, and who also had suffered serious frostbite, had returned home. When Krinov reached Vanavara he was approached by Lyuchetkan who said that he wanted to go to the "place where the fire fell down." Considering Lyuchetkan's earlier fear of entering the area, Krinov was surprised but welcomed him.

Kulik finally gave up drilling on March 1 when his boring pipes reached their limit of 30 meters. His meteorite still had not been struck. Two additional holes were drilled, but revealed nothing but spring-flood water. During the drilling of Hole #3 the small drill hut that sheltered the workers from the elements caught on fire and the drill apparatus was destroyed. On March 16, Krinov, Lyuchetkan, and three workmen left Kulik and two workmen to return to Leningrad with crates of scientific samples.

Krinov's report convinced the Academy to provide more funds for continued drilling during the 1930–1931 season. The Academy also approved one airplane to do the aerial survey that Kulik was so anxious to have. When the survey was completed in June, the pilot was to fly Kulik out so that he might return to Leningrad.

While waiting for the arrival of the airplane, Kulik shifted his attention from the Suslov crater to the Southern Swamp, where he felt that the parent meteorite lay buried. He also continued detailed meteorological observations, studies of the frozen peat for meteorite splinters, and studies of birds of the area. This last activity is rather interesting and reveals Kulik as a thorough investigator. One day while Yuriy and I were chatting at Kulik's work table at the Base Camp, Yuriy told me the following about Kulik:

"Roy, you must understand that in Russia Kulik is still a scientific legend and much honored. So much has been written about him, some of it exaggerated to make the legendary Kulik even bigger than life and some of it even fictionalized, to the disappointment of our scientific community. I will give you one example. It involves the incident when Kulik was told that escaped convicts were out to kill him. One writer, whom I will not name, exaggerated the event by saying that Kulik had discovered gold and that the convicts found him and fired bullets around his head, but he fought them off. Fiction!

"What I am about to tell you now, about his collecting birds, is not generally known, and as a researcher into Kulik's life I believe it to be true, not just part of the Kulik legend. Kulik's laboratory and study were in the large cabin behind where we are now sitting. It is where he slept also. As you saw this morning, bottles of some of his chemicals still rest on the shelves where he left them, as well as equipment from his photographic laboratory. And there were the many birds that Kulik had collected, examined, and skinned, and some of them he

Kulik's combination bedroom, laboratory, and office at his Base Camp. Photographic and other chemicals used by him are on the shelves where he last left them, and his small desk has remained undisturbed.   PHOTO BY GALLANT

mounted in lifelike poses. But he did not intend these bird specimens to be exhibited in a museum. Then why did he collect them? He cut open the crop of each bird—that little sac where the bird stores stones that grind its food before digesting it. He was interested in those stones. Since the birds peck stones out of the peat, Kulik thought that their crops might contain tiny fragments of meteorites. I tell you, Kulik overlooked nothing. Little by little, I have come to know many things about him by studying materials he left at this site, materials which I have discovered, assembled, and catalogued over the years of my going on these expeditions. Yes, this fact about Kulik's study of birds, and which has never been described anywhere, must be true. I am convinced of it."

On June 7 a messenger arrived at the Base Camp to tell Kulik that he was needed in Kezhma because the airplane assigned to do the aerial survey would soon arrive. In mid-July, Kulik was on hand to meet it. Day after day they waited for the low overcast sky to clear, but it didn't. Not a single photograph was taken. Discouraged and annoyed, Kulik packed up and on July 19 left Kezhma with two workmen and returned to the Base Camp once again. By this time, there had been so many workmen and scientific investigators trooping back and forth between Kezhma, Vanavara, The Dock, and the Base Camp that the local Tungus had overcome their earlier superstitious fear of entering Ogdy's enchanted land.

Through the remainder of the summer and until mid-September, Kulik reexamined his ideas and finally concluded that the Suslov "crater" was not a crater and that he would never find a meteorite stuck in its frozen basement. He further began to suspect that none of the other circular formations in the peat bogs contained meteorite fragments. By the time he returned to Leningrad in mid-October Kulik had refocused his thinking, strongly suspecting that "the real meteorite craters," and parent object, lay deep beneath the carpet of sphagnum moss in the Southern Swamp. He knew that his next task was to investigate the swamp by intensive drilling. He also must continue to press for an aerial survey.

According to Yuriy, during the summer of 1930 some of the workers had sent false reports to the local Communist party officials in Krasnoyarsk accusing Kulik of incompetence, which disturbed Kulik deeply because it could complicate his attempts at further expeditions. This, coupled with the physical hardships he had suffered and the negative results of the past difficult months, seriously affected Kulik, then age forty-seven. Yuriy added that in mid-October "Kulik returned to Leningrad with gray hair and ruined health."

In 1933 an astronomical group meeting in Cambridge, England wrote to the Soviet government and requested that an American group of researchers be allowed to conduct the aerial survey Kulik so much wanted. The government's reply was a strong *no*: "The fall of the Tunguska meteorite took place on the territory of the USSR and the search for it is the concern of Soviet scientists." That same year Kulik traveled from Leningrad to the Base Camp by himself in order to collect newly fallen meteorite dust from the snow surface.

KULIK'S LAST EXPEDITIONS

Kulik was not to return to Tunguska for another seven years. In May 1937 he was sent to Vanavara to direct his long-awaited aerial survey of the entire region, but the seaplane did not arrive until July 12. On one of the early flights, with Kulik and the photographer aboard, the plane crashed as the pilot brought it down for a landing on the Stony Tunguska River. Fortunately all survived unhurt. After the plane was repaired, the survey had to be postponed twice more because of bad weather.

It wasn't until June and July of 1938 that a survey was actually made, but by this time of year the young leaves of the trees had begun to grow and conceal much of the ground so that in many places the tree-fall pattern was hard to read. Kulik stayed in Tunguska until late October, planning to rephotograph certain sections after the autumn leaves fell, but once again bad weather prevented completion of the survey. He then returned to Leningrad. Although the aerial survey was incomplete, it did confirm ground observations of the radial pattern of fallen trees, but it failed to confirm Kulik's belief that the Southern Swamp marked the epicenter of the explosion.

On his last expedition, in 1939, Kulik returned to examine

the Southern Swamp. His group of eight reached the Base Camp on August 12 and immediately began to bore through the peat in numerous places in the sprawling swamp. Outside the swamp area the ground was layered with peat on top, then a mineral layer, and a mud bottom. Within the swamp, however, there was no such layering, only a chaos of peat, soil, and mud without a consistent pattern. Further, Kulik discovered numerous channels within the mud, all draining off in the direction of the Churgim Creek. He interpreted these observations as evidence of the meteorite's impact. Experts in swamp studies later were to refute Kulik's conclusions and say that the chaotic makeup of the Southern Swamp was natural and not unusual for the region.

Although the Academy of Sciences had approved Kulik's return to Tuguska in 1940 to conduct an extensive magnetic survey of the Southern Swamp, the expedition was canceled due to the Germans' military activity that led to World War II. Even though several highly respected scientists, in Russia and abroad, had expressed suspicion that an object other than a meteorite had been the cause of the 1908 explosion, Kulik was not swayed and fully believed that one day a huge iron mass would be found concealed at the bottom of the Southern Swamp.

Despite conflicting opinions over what caused the Tunguska event, Kulik continued to enjoy the respect of the international scientific community. This was reflected at home at the December 27 meeting of the Soviet Academy of Sciences in resolutions recognizing "the considerable achievements of Kulik and his group...in elaborating a technique for finding the possible point at which the meteorite fell [and noting] in particular the great persistence and enthusiasm shown by Kulik personally over many years in searching for the place where the Tunguska meteorite fell [and Kulik's] persistence and enthusiasm that led to the recent concrete advance in our knowledge of the subject."

July 5, 1941 brought a turn of events. The Nazis invaded Russia and Kulik joined the Moscow People's Militia. The Academy of Sciences tried to persuade Kulik not to risk his life by joining the volunteer military unit. He was an important scientist and Russia needed him alive. But as he was strong willed about his meteorite, he was equally strong willed about serving in the defense of his mother Russia. October found Kulik fighting in the front lines. He was wounded in the leg and taken prisoner by the advancing Nazis. In April of the following year, the month he usually arrived in Vanavara, the father of meteoric science died of typhus, despite the attempts of German and Russian doctors to save him. He was buried in the local cemetery in the town of Spas-Demensk in the Smolensk district of Russia. He was fifty-eight years old. An asteroid, a crater on the far side of the Moon, and a street in Vanavara today bear Kulik's name.

WHAT WAS IT?

*I*n 1946 a bizarre event refocused world attention on the mysterious explosion that devastated the Tunguska region on that June morning of 1908. And it was to spark new scientific, as well as popular, interest in the nature of the explosion. A backdrop for this controversial—perhaps "inflammatory" is a better word—idea had been provided in 1945 when the United States exploded the first atomic bomb 1,800 feet above the Japanese city of Hiroshima on August 6.

The man to touch off heated controversy over the Tunguska event was Aleksander Kazantsev, a forty-year-old engineer who had graduated from the Tomsk Technological Institute in 1930, at the time Kulik was probing the Southern Swamp. But Kazantsev had another calling for which he had become better known. He was a talented writer of tales of science fiction and fantasy. In 1936 he had won first prize in a national science fiction film scenarios competition. Kazantsev the engineer was thoroughly familiar with Kulik's expeditions and had read detailed descriptions of the flattened and scorched taiga, the oval "craters," and the telegraph-pole forest in the central region of the explosion.

As part of a Soviet team, Kazantsev had visited Hiroshima after the atomic bomb explosion to examine the devastation, and what he saw there excited his imagination as a spinner of tales. Just as the Tunguska forest had been scorched and felled by the cosmic visitor, virtually all the buildings and other structures outward from ground zero in Hiroshima had been scorched and flattened—except for one curious scene. A few hundred meters from the ground zero point there stood a miniature "telegraph-pole" forest, a small cluster of trees stripped of their branches.

EXPLORERS FROM MARS?

Additional similarities between Hiroshima and Tunguska led Kazantsev to write a science fiction story in which Kulik's meteorite was transformed into a Martian spaceship with a nuclear reactor engine that blew up over the desolate Siberia taiga. Later he was to embellish this scenario to fit new thinking about the Tuguska explosion. The Martians, he said, had come in search of water for their dried-up world and had been examining nearby Lake Baikal, Earth's deepest and largest body of fresh water, containing 20 percent of the planet's fresh water.

When Kazantsev's story was published in the Russian science fiction magazine *Around the World (Vokrug Sveta)* in 1946, it caught the attention not only of the public, but of scientists as well. Had Kazantsev not been highly respected among the scientific community, his fairy-tale account probably would have been dismissed with a giggle. But he did not end his tale there. He wrote further accounts in which he applied his considerable scientific knowledge to graphically describe the effects of a nuclear explosion over the Tunguska forest. In the eyes of some, his fictionalized accounts had merited the dignity of an alternative "hypothesis."

While the public tended to respond to this new nuclear hypothesis with enthusiasm, many members of the scientific community responded with indignant condemnation. Virtually every important astronomer in the then Soviet Union published an article criticizing Kazantsev's views, which he had spent ten years refining and publicizing. In 1958 his most elaborate publication appeared, an article entitled "A Guest from the Cosmos." And his 1963 book by the same title had as its theme the visitation of a Martian spaceship powered by a nuclear engine that blew up.

Twenty-six years later, in 1989, a group of some half dozen Japanese members of the UFO organization *Sakura,* "a special UFO research corps," was invited to join the first International Tunguska Expedition with the help of then President Mikhail Gorbachev. According to Kathy, who was a member of that expedition, "the Japanese tried to convince all the scientists that the 1908 explosion had been caused when the nuclear engine of a Japanese spaceship blew up. They said that the spaceship had left Japan two thousand years earlier and was returning home, but it somehow missed the runway by about 6,500 kilometers!"

In ordinary times most scientists simply would have shrugged off Kazantsev's fantasy as not even being nutworthy. But the postwar years were not ordinary times for Soviet science. A new breed of scientist, whose skills had been sharpened with the technology that grew out of World War II, became increasingly suspect of Kulik's meteorite and began to search for alternative causes of the Tunguska event. Oddly enough, the seed of one such viable cause was provided by a most unlikely source—Kazantsev. According to Academician Vasiliev, "Kazantsev had the explosion occurring not on the surface but at a certain height above the ground," a notion now universally accepted by modern research into the event. His spaceship fantasy also raised the question: "If the explosion had been a nuclear one, could it have been a *natural* phenomenon?" In other words, could it have been some unknown state of matter entering Earth's atmosphere?

EXPEDITIONS RESUMED—AND THREE SURPRISES

The controversy stirred up by Kazantsev seems to have played at least some part in persuading the Academy of Sciences to resume the Tunguska expeditions. But the strongest argument to do so came from one A. A. Yavnel, who in 1957 examined soil specimens that Kulik had brought back in 1929 and 1930. Yavnel reported that the samples contained small globules of magnetite and meteoric dust remarkably similar to meteoric materials from the famous Sikhote-Alin iron meteorite fall of 1947, second in size only to the Tunguska event in recorded history. He concluded that the Tunguska meteorite belonged to the iron class.

The Academy quickly organized a new Tunguska expedition for the summer of 1958. It was to be led by the Russian geochemist Kirill Florensky. Kirill achieved scientific prominence in the USSR, as had his famous father Professor P. Florensky who died in one of Stalin's concentration camps. The 1958 expedition included an impressive group of experts. In addition to Florensky, there was an astronomer, a mineralogist, a soils expert, a physicist, a chemist, and a second geochemist, plus several laboratory assistants and workmen. By this time twenty years had passed since the previous expedition and fifty years since the explosion. The expedition had two goals. One was to collect and analyze numerous peat samples from different locations within the epicenter region for telltale meteoric particles. The soil sampling program was carried out in an area of more than 1,000 square kilometers where the forest had been destroyed. Samples were taken at 5-kilometer intervals but were more closely spaced in the central region. The other goal was to begin work on mapping the area of felled trees. Florensky, like Krinov, was a firm believer in Kulik's meteorite theory. Meanwhile the controversy flared. The opposing view was held by those who favored a nuclear hypothesis or, more likely, some other above-ground explosion. But what kind of explosion?

On returning to Moscow, Florensky had a new map drawn up on the basis of the expedition's new topographical survey. The survey confirmed his suspicion that the epicenter was located not in the Southern Swamp, but on its western border. Here was important new evidence that the Southern Swamp could not be Kulik's meteorite crater. And imagine his surprise, and further disappointment, when examination of the eighty soil samples failed to agree with Yavnel's claim that Kulik's 1929–1930 samples contained fragments of nickel and other metallic particles implicating an iron meteorite. As it turned out, the Kulik samples examined by Yavnel accidentally had been mixed with samples from the Sikhote-Alin site when they were stored by the Committee on Meteorites. With that discovery the mystery of the remarkable similarity between the Kulik and Sikhote-Alin samples was solved.

While Florensky, Krinov, and the highly reputable investigator V. Fesenkov continued to support the meteorite hypothesis, they agreed the meteorite had exploded and disintegrated while still above the ground. They further agreed that Kulik's oval bog "craters" were nothing more than natural formations, a notion that soil scientists had suggested earlier.

Another important, and surprising, finding that came out of the 1958 expedition was that tree growth within the devastated area since 1908 had been much faster than tree growth outside the area. Trees that began growing after the 1908 explosion should have reached heights of about 8 meters by 1958. Instead, they had towered to heights of 17 to 22 meters. Botanists and other investigators up to the present time still are unable to account for this accelerated growth, and they continue to search for its cause.

In 1960 Fesenkov defected from the ranks of the meteorite enthusiasts. Meanwhile, scientists had come to realize that if a solution to the Tunguska riddle was to be found, the effort would require experts of many different disciplines, including botanists, geneticists, specialists in remote sensing, and physicians, among others. Accordingly, a number of new and informal groups began to work on the problem. The most significant among them was the one formed in 1958 in Tomsk. Called the Interdisciplinary Independent Expedition (IIE), it led to the formation of the Committee on Meteorites and Cosmic Dust of the Siberian Branch of the Soviet (now Russian) Academy of Sciences.

The first expedition of the IIE was held in 1959–1960 and was led by G. F. Plekhanov. One of the goals was to verify, or refute, a nuclear cause of the explosion. For the first time the soil and vegetation in the region of the epicenter were analyzed for traces of radioactivity. Plekhanov's group claimed that "in the center of the catastrophe, radioactivity is one and a half to two times higher than it is 30 or 40 kilometers away from the center." In addition, those who argued for the nuclear hypothesis cited eyewitness accounts of "radiation burns" found on certain of the surviving reindeer in the form of "scabs that had never appeared before the fire came."

One of the IIE's major efforts, over a period of nearly thirty years, was mapping the area of forest destruction, which was begun in 1958 by Florensky. This important work gradually enabled investigators to estimate the force of the 1908 explosion, its altitude, and certain other aspects of the blast.

METEOROIDS AND MICROSPHERULES

It was Florensky's idea that a search for microscopic particles of cosmic matter might lead to the identity of the Tunguska object. Accordingly, expeditions conducted in 1960 through 1962 collected more than 130 soil samples over an area of some 15,000 square kilometers. Florensky was assisted by a number of coworkers, among them the geologist B. Vronsky and members of the IIE. They collected and examined two kinds of microspherule pellets—magnetite and silicate. When separated and counted, they discovered that for each magnetite spherule there were about fifteen silicate spherules. In some cases a smaller magnetite spherule was found embedded within a silicate spherule, which showed that both were formed at the same time. Where did the spherules come from, and how were they formed?

When a meteoroid that is part iron and part rock burns its way down through Earth's atmosphere, its surface layers keep melting until there is nothing left, or until what remains of it strikes the ground. During the fiery fall, the melted matter— magnetite and silica—is blown off by strong air currents. It then forms a spray of microspherules that cool, solidify, and drift to the ground. Such microspherules make up the dust trails left behind those large exploding meteoroids called bolides.

Did the discovery of microspherules over the epicenter region prove that the Tunguska object was a meteorite, as Kulik had presumed? It so happens that each year several thousand meteorites the size of golf balls and tennis balls fall to the ground. In addition, each day from 20 to 400 tons of meteoric "dust" and micrometeorites rain down on Earth. So virtually all of Earth's surface, including the ocean beds, contains a "background" concentration of microspherules. The question that immediately comes to mind, or that should come to mind, is "Did the Tunguska epicenter contain a higher concentration of microspherules than the normal background concentration found outside the epicenter region? And if it did, does that *prove* that the cosmic visitor was a meteorite?"

Life seldom being as simple as we would like it to be, we must now complicate matters. According to Krinov, comet dust also sprays Earth's surface with the same kinds of microspherules that were dispersed unevenly over the Tunguska epicenter. So we must now ask the next question.

COULD IT HAVE BEEN A COMET?

As early as the 1930s some astronomers had begun to wonder if the 1908 cosmic visitor could have been a comet, as had been considered earlier by Kulik. Among them was the world's leading authority on comets, Fred L. Whipple of Harvard University. Others were the American astronomer Harlow Shapley and the Russian comet authority I. S. Astapovich. Whipple has portrayed comets as "dirty snowballs." Another astronomer describes these ghostly visitors as being "about as close to nothing as something can get." More recently, space probe investigations of comets on the move have portrayed them as "frozen mudballs," since some appear to contain more dust than ice.

Comets are balls of spongy ice mixed with rock dust, matter left over from the time the Solar System formed some 4.6 billion years ago. Billions of them are thought to be held in cold storage in an immense sphere, called the Oort cloud, which is wrapped around the Solar System at a distance of a few trillion kilometers. Jan H. Oort, the Dutch astronomer after whom the cloud was named, thinks there may be 100 billion comets making up his balloonlike swarm. And there seem to be still other comets in orbit beyond Pluto in another swarm called the Kuiper belt, after the astronomer G. P. Kuiper. If so, there is a

Comet Ikeya-Seki, as photographed October 29, 1965 by the Lick Observatory, University of California. As their ices are heated by the Sun, many comets develop tails several millions of kilometers long. The gases of the tail are pushed from the comet's head by radiation pressure of the Sun as the comet rounds the Sun on its brief visit. COURTESY: LICK OBSERVATORY

superabundance of cosmic missiles out there that have been targeting Earth and the other planets for eons.

Every once in awhile a distant passing star's gravitation pull grabs a comet from the Oort cloud and flings it on a long journey in toward the Sun. As the comet nears the Sun, the loose lump of rock dust and ice forming the comet's nucleus is heated and some of the ices boil off, forming a cocoon of gas called the coma. The coma swells into a ball extending up to a million kilometers or so out from the nucleus. The nucleus itself may be as small as only a kilometer or so in diameter, or it may be 100 kilometers across. In ages past, comets were called the "terrible stars," "death-bringing stars," and "hairy stars." They were "hairy" because of their long tails. The tails are composed of gases pushed out from the coma by pressure of the Sun's solar wind, a continuous gale of atomic particles cast off by the Sun. As recently as about one hundred years ago, people dreaded comets, thinking of them as messengers of doom that announce widespread disaster in the form of disease or war. Today we dread them for their potential of colliding with Earth and raising global havoc.

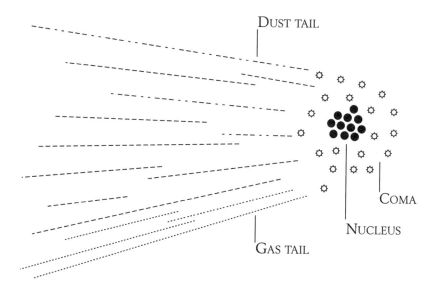

Comets are a mixture of rock dust and ice. At the center is the spongy nucleus that may be from about one to 80 kilometers across. As a comet approaches the Sun, the Sun's heat vaporizes some of the comet's ices. A cocoon of gases called the coma then forms around the nucleus. Some of the comet's gases are pushed out into a long tail composed of coma gases and rock dust.

By about 1960 the Russian investigator Fesenkov had written a number of articles that favored the comet hypothesis. More recently the Russian isotopic cosmic chemist Evgeniy Kolesnikov, of Moscow University, has become the chief investigator of the comet hypothesis, which, he says, most scientists favor today.

I visited Kolesnikov in his Moscow laboratory and later interviewed him in Tunguska during our summer expedition. "I became involved in the Tunguska investigations more than twenty years ago," he began. "At the time my colleagues and I were building devices to investigate the possible danger of radiation for cosmonauts in space. To do this our group investigated the radioactivity of meteorites. We measured the radioactivity levels of two different isotopes [forms] of the element argon— argon^{37} and argon^{39}.

"It occurred to me that I could use these same devices to check the antimatter hypothesis [see page 118] as well as the nuclear hypothesis of the Tunguska explosion. Knowing the power of the explosion, and its height above the ground, it would be easy to calculate the level of radioactive argon^{39} that should be found in the soil and upper layers of the basalt rocks of the epicenter region. My equipment was about one hundred times more sensitive than it needed to be for this task, so I could be certain of my findings. I did not find argon^{39} in any of the soil samples of basalt rocks brought to me, so I was able to say that the explosion could not have been a nuclear explosion, or one caused by antimatter."

I next asked what had led him to support the comet hypothesis. He said that he has a substantial body of data supporting a cometary origin of the Tunguska event. Part of that data includes comet matter found in peat (sphagnum) from the epicenter region. He then described the peat samples he has been studying over the years. The sphagnum plant (*Sphagnum fuscum*) takes its nutrient elements from the air rather than

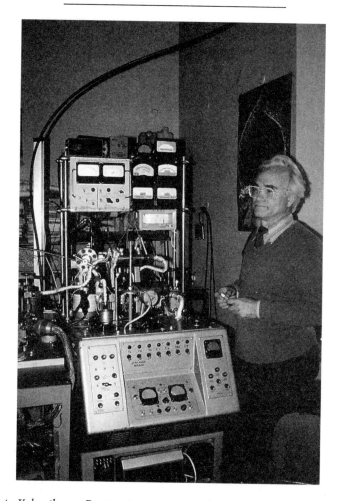

Evgeniy Kolesnikov, a Russian isotopic cosmic chemist of Moscow University, is the leading supporter of a cometary origin of the object that exploded over central Siberia in 1908. He has been involved in Tunguska investigations for more than 20 years. He is seen here in his Moscow laboratory.   PHOTO BY GALLANT

from the ground through roots. So any minerals and microscopic matter falling on the plant's living upper parts are incorporated into the plant. Every year the lower part of the plant dies as a new segment of stem grows. After each year's growth a little knot forms and marks that year's growth region of the stem. So by counting the knots down the stem the investigator can work all the way back to the 1908 layer in a sample block of peat. Chemical analysis of that layer of peat then reveals the abundance of this or that nutrient, or microspherules, that the plant concentrated in its tissues during the year. Comparing one year's growth layer with that of a higher or lower layer then provides a year-by-year record of the amounts of matter the plant took up from the environment.

"Although I didn't find any argon[39] in the soil and sphagnum samples I examined," Kolesnikov continued, "my colleagues [S. Golenetzky, for one] and I did find relatively high concentrations of silicate microspherules of unusual composition in the 1908 layer. At first we thought that these particles might be cometary matter released during the explosion, but it now seems more likely that these microspherules are not cosmic dust particles but were formed during the forest fires set by the 1908 explosion. Sometimes the 1908 layer also is marked by ash that settled on surviving vegetation during and after the fire."

Billy P. Glass, of the planetology branch of the Goddard Space Flight Center (NASA), agrees, saying that "none of the [silicate microspherules] seems to have compositions similar to the silicate portion of any major meteorite group." Whatever the source of the silicate microspherules, in 1908 there was a marked increase of them in the Tunguska epicenter region.

Another of Kolesnikov's projects was a layer-by-layer study of peat samples to learn if the 1908 layer contained higher concentrations of certain chemical elements associated with cosmic matter. In the peat sample taken not far from the Suslov "crater" he and his colleagues found relatively high concentrations of a number of light and volatile elements, including bromine, zinc, rubidium, and lead. "Because comets contain many such volatile elements," he said, "we are convinced that fallout from part of a comet's nucleus enriched the peat where our Suslov 'crater' sample was taken." He said that there was further evidence of the cosmic origin of the high concentrations of volatile elements in the sample. That evidence was the presence of lead isotopes found in the 1908 layer that differed from lead isotopes found in higher or lower layers of the sample, or in the surrounding soils or basalt rock. "Although extremely accurate," Kolesnikov added, "unfortunately, the kind of analyses we did are very time and labor consuming. For instance, for this one project we did about three thousand tests for different elements, and it took us more than two years."

Kolesnikov explained that you cannot dig just anywhere and expect to find telltale signs of cosmic dust at the 1908 level of peat samples: "My opinion is that the comet matter was dispersed unevenly," in a shotgun pattern rather than as an even rainfall. Krinov also supports a shotgun pattern of the blast, whatever its causes. As an example, he cites two sections of forest situated close to each other. While all the trees out of one section had been felled, trees in the other section were not touched by the blast. He also pointed out that within the larger epicenter area there are local and smaller epicenters of felled trees. Kulik had identified four such smaller epicenters, which would have been in keeping with the eyewitness statements that the explosion had sounded like a cannonade, a series of explosions, each creating its own miniepicenter and local concentration of cosmic matter. "That is why I think it's necessary to explore many locations in order to discover places containing a large content of the dispersed cosmic matter," Kolesnikov said.

Despite the hard work involved, Kolesnikov feels that proof of the identity of the Tunguska object will come from a continued collection and study of cosmic dust dispersed over the epicenter region and a study of isotopes of various elements found in the 1908 peat layers. He says that the most

Alyona Boyarkina, a senior scientific researcher at Tomsk State University in Siberia, is a veteran of 34 expeditions to Tunguska. Among her work is mapping the area of trees felled by the 1908 explosion, collecting thousands of soil, peat, and snow samples for analysis for cosmic dust, and the study of the magnetic properties of the soils in and around the epicenter region of the blast.

PHOTO BY GALLANT

telling isotopes are carbon[12] and carbon[13], hydrogen and deuterium, and nitrogen[14] and nitrogen[15], since comets contain those elements in especially high concentrations. He and his German colleague, Dr. Tatiana Bottger of Leipzig University, have measured isotopic anomalies of carbon and hydrogen in peat samples from the epicenter region. As this book was being prepared for publication, samples of peat taken under Kolesnikov's supervision during the 1992 expedition were being analyzed for isotope concentrations in his laboratory in Moscow and in laboratories in Germany and England.

OTHER LINES OF RESEARCH

Among other distinguished scientists on the 1992 expedition was Alyona Boyarkina, a senior scientific researcher of Tomsk University. She is a veteran of thirty-four expeditions and the author of more than one hundred scholarly papers about the Tunguska event. Over the years, beginning with the second expedition of the IIE in 1960–61, she has devoted more time in her research into the Tunguska explosion than did Kulik or any other investigator. For a number of years she took part in mapping the area of felled trees, and she has collected thousands of soil, peat, and snow samples for analysis for cosmic dust.

"More recently," she said, "I have been investigating the magnetic properties of the soils in and around the epicenter region. We have collected hundreds of small cubes from ten different locations and have marked their north-facing sides. In the laboratory we will measure their magnetic fields and compare them with the standard magnetic field in this area. We will then be able to identify any differences in the magnetic properties. You should understand that during the fall of the Tunguska object there was a strong magnetic disturbance, and my present work is to measure the exact nature of that disturbance."

When I asked Boyarkina if she thought her line of research might one day explain what caused the 1908 explosion, she answered, "Not straight away, perhaps. But there are numerous hypotheses. For instance, let's take the plasma hypothesis, one suggesting that a fragment of the Sun's hot gases was hurled toward Earth. According to the hypothesis, if a piece of that plasma collided with the atmosphere there should be strong magnetic disturbances imprinted in the soil. So my research, by itself, cannot answer the question. But it can help support or perhaps contradict certain hypotheses."

Boyarkina's work represents but one of the many pieces of the Tunguska jigsaw puzzle. When carefully fitted in place with other pieces supplied by other researchers, the broader picture of the Tunguska puzzle should one day emerge.

The youngest researcher in our 1992 group was a German scholar named Karin Junghans, an authority in remote sensing. Before coming to Tunguska she had studied satellite (Landsat) photographs of the Tunguska region in an attempt to identify vegetation peculiarities. She states her goal as "to compare the results of my interpretation of the satellite images with the actual landscape and areas of peculiar vegetation growth." Junghans's remote sensing studies can reveal those areas of accelerated vegetation growth that occurred right after the 1908 explosion. As a result, her work provides an important new perspective on biological aspects of the Tunguska event. And that is another small but significant piece of the puzzle.

COULD IT HAVE BEEN AN ASTEROID?

In 1992 three American researchers—C. F. Chyba, P. J. Thomas, and K. J. Zahnie—worked out a computer model suggesting that the Tunguska object was a stony asteroid, the most common class of meteorites. The object, Chyba claims, was about 60 meters in diameter, or about half the size of a football field.

His model paints this picture of the asteroid's entry into the atmosphere and its disintegration: It enters at a speed of about 15 kilometers a second (about 34,000 miles an hour). Its great speed compresses and piles the air ahead of it. But just behind the asteroid is a near vacuum, which sets up a huge pressure difference across the asteroid. And the pressure difference increases as the object plunges into denser regions of the atmosphere. The rocky asteroid envisioned by Chyba would next tend to crumble and flatten out, or "pancake," as it became unable to maintain its shape against the increasing pressure difference. This spreading out increased the atmospheric drag even more until suddenly the object exploded like a bomb.

Chyba dismisses the comet hypothesis, saying that comets are not dense enough to survive for long in the atmosphere and so they self-destruct at very high altitudes, so high that "they are scarcely noticed at the surface." Astronomer Zdenek Sekanina, writing in the September 1983 *Astronomical Journal*, agrees. A comet fragment behaving as the Tunguska object behaved, he said, would have encountered almost one thousand times more air resistance than usually destroys cometary meteors—convincing evidence that the Tunguska object had to be a much denser object.

How do Chyba and his colleagues of the asteroid model account for the well-documented "light nights" of June 30 and the following few days? They theorize that the fireball explosion hurled large amounts of water into the upper atmosphere. On cooling, the water droplets froze as ice crystal clouds that were then dispersed by the global circulation of the air. The resulting noctilucent clouds then produced the light nights.

H. J. Melosh, of the Lunar and Planetary Laboratory of the University of Arizona, calls the Chyba computer model "relatively crude" and adds that "there is still work to be done on the physics of Tunguska-like explosions." In the author's opinion, we know far too little about comets to flatly dismiss a cometary origin of the Tunguska object. We have yet to send a space probe to sample the nucleus of a "live" comet to find out about its composition and structure. Further, we have no hard evidence that all comets are alike.

Two other American researchers also favor the asteroid model. They are Jack G. Hills, of the Los Alamos National Laboratory, and M. Patrick Goda, of Wabash College. In the March 1992 issue of the *Astronomical Journal* they write that the Tunguska object was an asteroidal fragment at least 80 meters in diameter that penetrated the atmosphere at 22 kilometers a second.

When Chyba's stony asteroid model was first published it stirred considerable interest among astronomers. What the article failed to point out, however, was that the well-known Russian investigator V. P. Korobeinikov had considered a stony asteroid model thirty years earlier, as had other Russian investigators in 1960, 1968, 1978, and 1989. In private correspondence with the author, Korobeinikov said that he found nothing new in Chyba's paper. He added, "In my opinion, we have to consider several suppositions—the object's flight through the atmosphere, its fracture, flight after fracturing and breaking up, shock wave system, radiation, ground effects, and so on. [I further feel that] the cometary hypothesis is one of the best from different scientific perspectives, although I do not reject the stony asteroid hypothesis." The fact is, he added, "the true study is not finished."

COULD IT HAVE BEEN ANTIMATTER?

Most physicists will tell you that there is a lot of matter out there in space the properties and behavior of which are unknown to us. That idea has led to a lot of the pseudoscience and speculation about the Tunguska event mentioned by Valentin Tsvetkov on the dedication page of this book. The

Russian geophysicist A. V. Zolotov echoed this idea in his statement that the Tunguska object "represents a new yet unknown, much more complicated phenomenon of nature than has been encountered up to this time." But what kind of "complicated phenomenon"?

Once again, American scientists unfamiliar with the wealth of data about the Tunguska site supported the idea that the complicated phenomenon was an "antirock," or a piece of antimatter, as mentioned earlier by Kolesnikov. (See page 110.) Physicists had earlier predicted the existence of antimatter. Its occurrence was confirmed in 1932 by Carl D. Anderson. Antimatter also might have been termed "oppositematter" since its atoms have electrical charges opposite those of ordinary matter. For instance, instead of having an electric charge of +1 as ordinary protons do, a proton of antimatter has an electrical charge of -1. When a proton of antimatter and a proton of ordinary matter collide, they annihilate each other and in the process produce other subatomic particles such as photons and pions.

In 1941 the American meteorite authority Lincoln La Paz was the first to suggest that the Tunguska object might have been a lump of antimatter. The Russian science fiction writer Kazantsev liked the idea, and even said that his Martian spaceship's engine might have been made of antimatter. A number of American scientists, as late as the mid-1960s, also liked the idea. They included Willard Libby, Clyde Cowan, and C. R. Atluri. But antiarguments soon spelled doom for the antimatter idea. For instance, it was argued that a lump of antimatter wouldn't survive the journey down through the atmosphere without being annihilated. Another objection was that if the antirock did somehow manage to survive and reach a height of 10 kilometers above the ground before exploding, it would produce large amounts of radioactive carbon[14]. Interestingly enough, traces of the radioactive carbon were found by several investigators in the 1909 ring of tree-ring samples. However, the most probable cause for the carbon's presence is not an antirock, but the simultaneous occurrence of two periods of especially strong solar activity.

COULD IT HAVE BEEN A BLACK HOLE?

In the late 1930s physicists with a special interest in astronomy had begun to speak of a strange state of matter that eventually became known as black holes.

All stars are kept shining as their hot core regions fuse hydrogen into helium and then helium into still heavier elements. These fusion reactions produce enormous amounts of light, heat, and other energy. After burning for millions or billions of years, all stars eventually use up their hydrogen fuel supply and must one day go out as their nuclear furnaces cool and die.

Extremely massive stars have core temperatures so high that their nuclear furnaces are able to forge atoms as heavy as iron. But that seems to be the limit. These stars, too, must one day burn themselves out. Such massive stars are represented by the extremely hot blue-white stars, like the giant star Sirius, which we see in the winter sky near the constellation Orion the Hunter. When these stars exhaust their fuel supply, a strange fate awaits them. The nuclear fires raging in the core of these very massive stars generate enormous pressure that keeps the star swollen up as a huge sphere of gases. When the nuclear fires go out and the core pressure falls, the star collapses in on itself until it is only a few kilometers in diameter. Earlier its diameter had been more than a hundred million kilometers.

Such a collapsed giant star becomes so dense and its gravity so strong that no energy—not even light—can escape from it. The star has become a black hole. A tablespoon of black hole matter is so dense that it weighs several billion tons. Black holes come in many sizes, according to the British physicist Stephen Hawking—from the size of enormous mountains to that of a flea. The smallest black holes are called "goblins." According to theory, a goblin the size of a small lemon contains as much matter as planet Earth. We are told that a goblin the size of a speck of dust would weigh more than a billion tons.

If the properties of black holes seem strange, their behavior will seem even stranger. A miniature black hole the size of a golf ball traveling 1,000 kilometers a second could pass through millions of kilometers of solid rock before slowing down.

By now you may have guessed that eventually someone would suggest that the Tunguska object was a black hole. And someone did. The black hole supposedly smashed into the Southern Swamp and just kept on going until it passed right on through the planet and out the other side, emerging out of the mid-Atlantic Ocean near the Azores. As in the case of antimatter, in 1973 two more American scientists, who seemed unaware of the masses of Tunguska data accumulated by Russian investigators over the years, proposed the black hole hypothesis. They were A. A. Jackson and Michael P. Ryan, of the University of Texas at Austin.

Jackson and Ryan imagined a goblin-sized object with the mass of a large asteroid traveling fast enough to penetrate the last 30 kilometers of Earth's atmosphere in about one second. The shock wave pushed before it supposedly caused all the damage. Writing in the British science magazine *Nature*, these researchers said that "since the black hole would leave no crater or material residue, it explains the mystery of the Tunguska event. It would enter the Earth, and the rigidity of rock would allow no underground shock wave. Because of its high velocity and because it loses only a small fraction of its energy in passing through the Earth, the black hole should very nearly follow a straight line through the Earth, entering at 30 degrees to the horizon and leaving through the North Atlantic in the region 40 to 50 degrees N, and 30 to 40 degrees W."

There are so many objections to this hypothesis that the expedition scientists I spoke with became irritated at the mere mention of the idea and shook their heads in frustration. Academician Vasiliev reflected their feelings and summarized their views: "If Jackson and Ryan had bothered to acquaint themselves with the geophysical materials published in Russia and America before publicizing their fantastic idea, they most likely would never have proposed it. Evidently the authors, in their naïveté, supposed that in 1908 such a cataclysmic event as a black hole exploding out of the North Atlantic Ocean would have gone unnoticed. However, the population of the eastern regions of Canada, Iceland, and southern Greenland was significant. Those people published newspapers and had meteorological stations and observatories, and there were dozens of vessels in the open ocean. Furthermore, a tsunami [giant destructive ocean wave] would have been generated. Under these circumstances the event could not possibly have gone unnoticed.

"If professional scientists indulge themselves in such liberties, you can imagine how readily such science fiction notions will be eagerly and gullibly seized by the mass media. For example, much publicity was given to the fantastic notion of T. Altov and V. Zhuravlev that the Tunguska event was caused by a laser ray fired by inhabitants of a distant planet in an attempt to communicate with Earth. Too often the mass media try to clothe such pseudoscientific notions with the respectability of science. The sad results are disoriented public opinion and complications in the further study of this complex natural phenomenon," Vasiliev concluded.

WHERE MATTERS STAND NOW

At the present time these five things about the Tunguska event are certain:

(1) The Tunguska puzzle has not been solved, despite misleading headlines that periodically appear in newspapers and popular science magazines. For example: STUDY FINDS ASTEROID LEVELED SIBERIAN AREA IN '08 (the *New York Times*); SCIENTISTS: 1908 BLAST NO MYSTERY (*Portland* [Maine] *Press Herald*); IN 1908 A SMALL ASTEROID EXPLODED OVER REMOTE SIBERIA, SOUNDING A WARNING ASTRONOMERS ARE JUST BEGINNING TO HEAR (*Astronomy Magazine*).

(2) Most investigators favor either a comet or an asteroid origin for the 1908 explosion, the cometary hypothesis being favored. As of this writing, the case definitely has not been closed.

(3) Had the Tunguska object come sailing into the atmosphere a short time later, it would have exploded over St. Petersburg, killed at least half a million people, and flattened the city virtually beyond recognition.

(4) Natural cosmic visitors immensely more destructive than the Tunguska object have collided with this planet countless times in Earth's past.

(5) More such objects are bound to come crashing into us again—and very likely with devastating consequences.

CHAPTER TEN

TARGET EARTH!

*T*he Tunguska "marvel" of 1908 commands more world attention today than it did a half century ago. Over the past seventy or so years the superblast has been publicized in hundreds of scientific papers, more than one thousand popular articles, more than sixty novels and nonfiction books, and numerous poems, motion pictures, and television programs. The bewitching aspect of each is the implied double question, "When and where will the next one strike? And how much damage will it cause?"

There are several reasons for the newfound fascination with what the National Aeronautics and Space Administration (NASA) has come to call "Near-Earth-Objects," or NEOs. One is that the world has grown space conscious. The agents of this turn of mind are a combination of highly popular space odyssey films and the spectacular scientific feats of the United States and Russian space exploration programs. Both have vastly enlarged our awareness of what is out there in the dark. Over the years scientists have found that there are untold numbers of uninvited cosmic visitors who have dropped in on us countless times in the past, and who will continue to call. But just when, we don't know. And there lies our fascination with these planet-crunching objects—comets and asteroids.

HITS AND MISSES

According to NASA, a 10-meter-diameter cosmic missile passes closer to us than the Moon's distance each day; and an object 100 meters across speeds past Earth at about the Moon's distance on the average of once a month. In January of 1991 a

Source: Geological Survey of Canada **EARTH'S GREATEST HITS**

Map shows the location of 139 large Earth craters made by comets and asteroids over the past thousands and millions of years. Some of the impacts affected life on a global scale. Because Earth is a geologically active planet, virtually all of its giant craters were long ago eroded away or covered over by vegetation.

MAP BY RICK BRITTON

Deep Bay Crater is a giant more than 15 kilometers across. It lies about 460 kilometers north of Prince Albert, Saskatchewan, Canada. First investigated in 1956, it is filled with water, the greatest depth of which is 220 meters. Its best preserved wall segment rises almost half a kilometer. Evidence gathered during investigations strongly points to a meteoritic fall.   Royal Canadian Air Force Photo

10-meter object missed Earth by only half the Moon's distance just twelve hours after astronomers spotted it.

As of this writing, the record closest approach of an asteroid came on December 9, 1994, when Asteroid $1994XM_1$, 13 meters in diameter, missed us by 100 kilometers. The previous closest approach was by Asteroid $1994ES_1$. In March 1994 it passed less than 150,000 kilometers from us. Asteroids in the range of 50 to several hundred meters may impact Earth every 200 to 300 years. But, according to Chyba, we don't have to

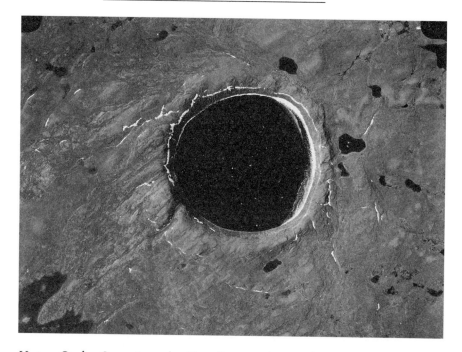

Ungava-Quebec Crater is another Canadian giant lying at the northwest end of Ungava Peninsula in Quebec, Canada. More than 3 kilometers in diameter, it is water-filled and reaches a depth of 361 meters. Its walls rise 100 meters above the surrounding rock desert. Thought to be between 3,000 and 15,000 years old, the crater seems to have been formed by a large meteorite plunging to the ground from a west-southwest direction. Small pond depressions around the main crater are thought to have been formed by meteorite fragments that traveled with the main object. ROYAL CANADIAN AIR FORCE PHOTO

worry about the house-size objects smaller than about 50 meters because they can't make it through the atmosphere without burning up—unless they happen to be iron rather than stony objects. The giants, those mountain-size objects one kilometer and more in diameter, are thought to collide with Earth on the average of once every 500,000 years. As one writer has put it, "We live in a cosmic shooting gallery." And the fact is that we do get hit, and more than we realize.

From 1975 to 1992 U.S. military satellites detected 136 high-altitude explosions with a force of 500 to 15,000 tons of high explosives—in effect, small atomic bombs. But our government decided to keep the information secret. Not until early in 1994 did they make the information public, and astronomers for the first time learned about the cosmic bombardments. They were informed that the objects entered the atmosphere at 16 to 48 kilometers a second, that they exploded 27 to 32 kilometers above Earth's surface, and that there probably were 10 times more events than were detected.

What about the supergiant asteroids measuring more than one kilometer in diameter? Tom Gehrels, of the University of Arizona, has been counting asteroids that come close enough to Earth to be a threat. He searches the sky through a 36-inch telescope on Kitt Peak, Arizona. In the late 1980s he and his group of sky watchers were spotting fifteen new asteroids a year "of the size that could eliminate human society," he reported. In 1992 the group spotted more than twice that number and they expect to be up to one hundred a year before the end of the 1990s. Over a period of four nights in 1990, the Jet Propulsion Laboratory's Eleanor Helin sighted three giant asteroids. One of them, which crosses Earth's orbit, is 30 kilometers in diameter. A collision with one that size would most likely wipe out most traces of life on the planet. The NASA group that is studying threats from asteroids estimates that there are between 1,000 and 4,000 one-kilometer objects that cross Earth's orbit. Of that estimated number the orbits of only about 150 are known. The NASA group further estimates that there are about 300,000 more 90-meter asteroids that cross Earth's orbit. But any catalog of cosmic intruders goes out of date almost as soon as it is revised.

In 1992 NASA invited more than a hundred scientists to take part in two workshops. The first, called "The Spaceguard Survey," dealt with scanning the skies for Earth-threatening asteroids and comets. The second was called "Near-Earth-Object Interception Workshop," and its report begins with these words: "In the last decade, there has been a major shift in the perception of potential hazards to human life from Earth-approaching cosmic objects. A vast increase in evidence linking large-scale extinctions of species to past impacts on the Earth has driven this increased concern. At the same time, there has been a great increase in the rate of discovery of near-Earth objects, including some which have made near passes by Earth."

The purpose of the second workshop was to propose ways of either destroying near-Earth objects that pose a threat before they can destroy us or of nudging them into an orbit that would take them safely out of Earth's path. In the next chapter we will return to those proposals. But first, what are asteroids, and what planetwide havoc have they raised in the past?

CASE OF THE MISSING PLANET

In the year 1772 the astronomer Johann Bode said that there was something amiss in the Solar System—a missing planet that should be in the "gap" between Mars and Jupiter. A group of German astronomers calling themselves "celestial police" began searching space between those two planets. On January 1, 1801, a planet was found, or so thought the Sicilian astronomer Giuseppi Piazzi who spotted a tiny object about where Bode had predicted the "missing" planet should be. It turned out to be a midget planet, or planetoid, only 1,000 kilometers in diameter, about one-third the Moon's size and several times smaller than its neighbor Mars. It was named Ceres.

The next year an even smaller companion planetoid was found. Named Pallas, it was only half as large as Ceres. By 1807 two more—Juno and Vesta—had been discovered. Juno has a

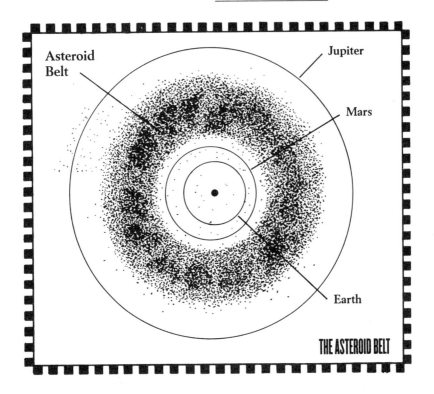

Asteroid Belt

Jupiter

Mars

Earth

THE ASTEROID BELT

As of September 1994, the positions of 5,531 asteroids were known. The asteroids are rock and metal fragments ranging from the size of golf balls to mountains. Most orbit in a belt between Mars and Jupiter, but there now seems to be a second belt closer to Earth.   DIAGRAM BY RICK BRITTON

diameter of 240 kilometers, and Vesta's diameter is 540 kilometers. Because of Vesta's size and light color, compared with the dark color of Ceres and Pallas, Vesta is the brightest planetoid and can be seen without a telescope. Astronomers have plotted the orbits of a few thousand of these objects, now called asteroids. But there are millions more, an estimated half million of which have a diameter of more than one kilometer.

HOW WERE THE ASTEROIDS FORMED?

Are the asteroids the remains of a smashed planet? Astronomers pondered that question for many years. Light-colored Eros tumbles along end-over-end like a kicked football. Pallas, dark and sphere shaped, is peppered with craters. And one named Hektor is a dumbbell-shaped double asteroid. In 1994 astronomers discovered that asteroid Ida, 60 kilometers

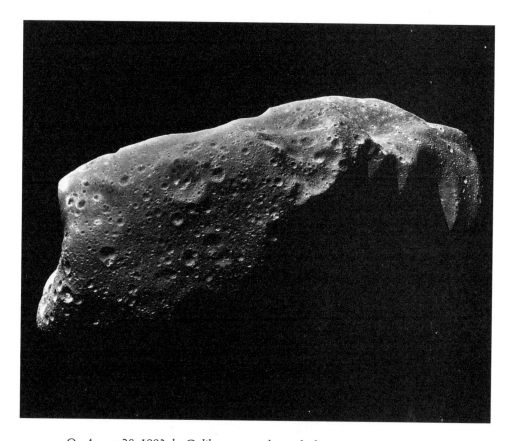

On August 28, 1993 the Galileo space probe made this mosaic image of the asteroid 243 Ida from an average distance of 3,500 kilometers. Only the second asteroid to be approached by a space probe, Ida is a giant about 52 kilometers long. Many craters are visible. Ida is thought to be a stony fragment (S-type asteroid) broken off a larger object during collision. NASA PHOTO

long, has a small moon named Dactyl, 1.4 kilometers in diameter. At one time astronomers wondered if a Mars-size planet gradually could have been pulled in ever closer to Jupiter by that planet's strong gravitation, and eventually shattered by Jupiter's powerful gravitational grip. The millions of pieces then would have remained in orbit as the swarm of asteroids we observe today.

One reason this theory of the asteroids' origin at first seemed attractive was that the dark asteroids appear to be mostly nickel and iron while the lighter ones are composed either of rocky matter or a combination of rock and iron-nickel. That is exactly what we might expect to find among the rubble of a shattered planet—chunks of metal from the planet's core, fragments of part-metal and part-rock from the planet's midregion, and pieces of rocky matter from the crustal material. As appealing as the idea seemed, astronomers came to abandon it. Most felt that Jupiter's strong gravitational influence would have prevented the original chunks of rock and rock-metal, out of which all the planets were formed, from ever fashioning a planet in the Mars-Jupiter "gap."

Over the years astronomers have discovered that the asteroid swarm is not neatly confined to a racetrack-shaped orbit between Mars and Jupiter. From time to time these objects smash into each other and shatter. Some of their pieces then bound away into highly eccentric, or elongated, orbits in a game of cosmic billiards. The eccentric orbits of a number of asteroids bring them close to Earth on a regular basis, crossing Earth's orbit. Nightly we see many of the smaller fragments burn up in Earth's atmosphere as sporadic meteors. Frictional heating, due to speeds of 15 to 70 kilometers a second, destroys most of them before they can strike the ground as meteorites. The larger and potentially dangerous intruders are called Apollo Objects, Earth-grazers, NEOs, and NEAs (Near-Earth Asteroids). They were designated Apollo Objects after the asteroid of that name.

Crusted-over dead comets, dried-up comets that have lost their ices, also are included as Apollo Objects.

Astronomers now estimate that there are between 5,000 and 10,000 NEOs with diameters of half a kilometer or more. They come in three classes: Amors, which cross the orbit of Mars and approach Earth's orbit; Atens, which orbit closer to the Sun than Earth but which may cross Earth's path; and the Apollos, which cross Earth's orbit to within a distance closer than the Moon. Half of all the known NEOs have been discovered within the last five years (of this writing), with two or three new ones being found each month. According to David I. Rabinowitz, of the University of Arizona, the large number of small NEOs suggests a second asteroid belt, one near Earth.

More than any other event in human history, the crash of Comet Shoemaker-Levy 9 into Jupiter in July 1994 drove home the realization of the destructive force of a large cosmic object smashing into a planet. Just one of the comet's twenty-one major pieces—Fragment G—released the force of at least six million megatons of energy. That amounts to six million tons of TNT. Think of it as the total energy released by the explosion of a Hiroshima-type atomic bomb once every second for ten years! The evidence about shoemaker-Levy 9 will continue to be sifted over for many months, or years. Early on, some astronomers began to suspect that the object wasn't a comet but a stony asteroid. Another suspicion was that the object might have been a dead comet whose ices had melted long ago, leaving only a spongelike skeleton of carbon and silicon.

During the seven-day period when Shoemaker-Levy 9's pieces were bombarding Jupiter, the United States House of Representatives Committee on Science, Space and Technology ordered NASA to work on a plan to detect errant comets or asteroids that might threaten destruction on Earth. NASA quickly responded by setting up the Near-Earth-Object Search Committee. As its head they appropriately named astronomer and comet-finder Eugene M. Shoemaker who had long urged the formation of such a group. Said Shoemaker of the Jupiter event: "If the comet had hammered Earth, it would have set off a global catastrophe."

EARTH'S GREATEST "MURDER" MYSTERY

Scientists find it convenient to separate Earth's 4.6 billion-year geologic history into smaller time units called periods. Geologic periods differ from one another depending on when certain kinds of plants and animals lived, when certain mountain ranges were thrust up, or when inland seas advanced over and then retreated from the continents from time to time. The period that interests us here began 138 million years ago and is called the Cretaceous Period. It lasted 72 million years, coming to a dramatic end about 66 million years ago. The name comes from the Latin word *creta*, meaning "chalk."

The Cretaceous was a time of mountain building. The Rocky Mountains of North America and the mighty Andes of South America were thrust up over millions of years. Although the continents familiar to us today had begun to take their present shapes, Cretaceous seas covered most of Europe, much of Asia, and nearly half of North America. During this period rivers and streams dumped nearly 3,500 meters of sediment onto the floor of the Gulf of Mexico. Flowering plants had become common by this time, as had giant sequoias. Sharks again became abundant after a long interval of decreased populations. Snakes made their first appearance on the evolutionary landscape, as did the first primitive mammals. The land was not to feel the footsteps of the first humans for another 136 million years, but it trembled with the heavy tread of those terrible lizards—the dinosaurs.

The dinosaurs had begun to evolve more than 70 million

years earlier. During the Cretaceous they lumbered, scampered, and ran over the land and sloshed and swam through the inland seas, but the close of the Cretaceous was to mark their end. Their wholesale extinction, along with thousands of other species of animals and plants, has long been Earth's greatest murder mystery. But over the last dozen years a growing body of evidence has tended to identify the culprit that brought about the mass extinctions that characterize the close of the Cretaceous.

In 1977 the father-and-son team Luis and Walter Alvarez, of the University of California, Berkeley, proposed the idea that a massive asteroid smashed into Earth, probably somewhere in the sea, and killed off the dinosaurs and many other groups of animals and plants. The object vaporized and sent an enormous plume of pulverized rock, dust, and gases high into the atmosphere. The cloud was spread by the global air circulation and for months it blocked out sunlight from most of the planet's surface. Green plants' ability to carry out photosynthesis was interrupted, triggering the widespread ecological collapse that produces wholesale extinctions. Between 60 and 80 percent of all species were wiped out.

What evidence did the Alvarez team have for their asteroid theory? Many scientists then seriously questioned the idea, but today many accept it.

In 1977 geologist Walter Alvarez was digging through the sedimentary rocks outside Gubbio, Italy. As he worked, he was puzzled by a sandwichlike layering of limestone. The bottom layer contained many tiny fossils and marked the upper level of rocks of the Cretaceous Period. On top of that layer was a half-inch-thick layer of dull red clay. And above the clay layer was a second layer of limestone that represented the earliest sediments laid down at the beginning of the next geological period, called the Tertiary Period. Alvarez noticed that the Tertiary limestone contained hardly any fossils. Scientists refer to this clay-layer division as the Cretaceous/Tertiary, or K/T, boundary. It was as if the life that had abounded in the late Cretaceous suddenly, in geological time at least, had been virtually snuffed out. The agent of doom, the Alvarezes suspected, might be hidden in that thin layer of red clay forming the filling of the K/T sandwich.

Walter Alvarez shipped samples of the rock back home and showed them to his father, a Nobel Prize-winning physicist. When the puzzling red clay layer was analyzed, everyone was surprised to find that it contained large amounts of the element iridium, a rare and hard silvery-white metal related to platinum and gold. Iridium is uncommon in Earth's crustal rock but occurs in higher concentrations deep within the planet. It also is known to occur in certain asteroids, in certain of their smaller cousins, meteoroids, and in comets and cosmic dust. The Alvarez sample turned out to contain thirty times more iridium than Earth's common crustal rocks. The question now was "How did the iridium-rich clay layer at the K/T boundary get there?"

The Alvarezes proposed that the explosion and vaporization of an iridium-rich extraterrestrial invader—a metallic asteroid—was the agent of catastrophe. When the asteroid struck and disintegrated, its iridium dust was blown skyward, was caught up in the global air circulation, and eventually settled onto the Cretaceous landscape virtually everywhere. Other scientists attracted to the cosmic-visitor idea suggested that the object might have been a comet some 10 kilometers in diameter. Whatever its nature, a cosmic visitor had been implicated.

WAS THE COSMIC-CULPRIT IDEA TESTABLE?

If an idea in science is to be taken seriously, it must be testable. Also, it should suggest certain predictions. The asteroid theory meets both requirements. For example, it predicts that the iridium-rich layer should be present in the K/T boundary not only in Italy, but everywhere on the planet where a column of sediments crossing the boundary is complete. Research over the last dozen years has shown the prediction to be true. Nearly every location tested has the expected iridium concentration— on land and beneath the sea floor, and from Montana to Denmark to Tunisia and in the northern and southern Pacific Ocean.

The asteroid impact theory meets other predictions as well. The K/T boundary layer should contain certain by-products of an explosive impact. It does. According to paleontologist David Jablonski of the University of Chicago, "Osmium, chromium, cobalt, and other elements are more abundant in [the K/T layer] than should be expected in Earth's crust." He also points out that telltale glasslike microspheres (microtektites) and shocked quartz grains characteristically formed during explosive impacts also occur in abundance in the K/T boundary layer.

Perhaps the most convincing evidence found to date is the discovery of a 66 million-year-old giant impact crater—the Chicxulub Crater—in the sea floor off the coast of Mexico's Yucatan Peninsula. It measures 300 kilometers across and is 9 kilometers deep. The asteroid thought to have made the crater must have measured at least 10 kilometers across and weighed hundreds of billions of tons. More recent evidence suggests that a second asteroid splashed down into the Pacific Ocean at just about the same time 2,000 kilometers east of Japan. That impact also produced microspheres that contain high levels of iridium. Researchers who have studied the ocean floor distribution of the microspheres estimate that the impacting object was about 2 kilometers in diameter. It is possible that additional objects, all members of a swarm, struck at the same time.

WHEN THE CHICXULUB ASTEROID STRUCK

Atmospheric scientists Ronald G. Prinn and Bruce Fegley, of the Massachusetts Institute of Technology, have worked out computer models that suggest what conditions could have been like after the Yucatan cosmic object struck: There would have been thick clouds of dust and smoke from fires that probably destroyed one-quarter of the planet's vegetation. A dense fog of nitrogen oxides would have helped blanket the planet in darkness lasting a year. All bodies of water would have been poisoned by metals released from soil and rock. Planetwide acid rains as corrosive as battery acid would have soaked the land and further poisoned the water.

Whether the cosmic visitor was an asteroid or a comet, according to Prinn and Fegley, the force of the explosion would have been greater than an explosion of all the nuclear weapons stored on the planet during the 1980s. The atmosphere would have been instantly heated, resulting in nitrogen oxides remaining as deadly pollutants for plants and air-breathing animals, including the dinosaurs. Deprived of sunlight, plants would have been the first to die, along with marine organisms living in shallow water. The acid rains would have dissolved the calcium-carbonate shells of water dwellers such as the spiral-shelled ammonites, which died out in large numbers at the end of the Cretaceous. But acid-resistant organisms, such as the silica-shelled diatoms, survived. Small land animals that burrowed, such as the early mammals, also would have been favored.

A number of scientists, including Niles Eldredge, a paleontologist at the American Museum of Natural History, feel that the Cretaceous extinctions were not a sudden affair, but that they had begun millions of years earlier and then somehow were speeded up during the late Cretaceous. S. M. Stanly of Johns Hopkins University agrees, saying that a comet impact late in the Cretaceous would have made an already bad situation truly awful. Says Eldredge, "We really are dealing with the [slow] collapse of ecosystems here." More evidence for such a gradual process has come from William Zinsmeister of Purdue University, who has studied Cretaceous extinction patterns on Seymour Island, near the Antarctic Peninsula. "In high latitudes, you just don't see the marked extinctions. . . . [Instead] you see gradual change, a gradual drop off," he said.

There have been other mass extinctions in Earth's geological past—at the end of the Cambrian Period (some 500 million years ago) and during the Upper Devonian Period (about 340 million years ago), to name only two. Those two periods are named after *Cambria*, the Roman name for Wales, and Devon in England. The most devastating mass extinction now seems to have occurred at the end of the Permian Period, some 245 million years ago, named after the province of Perm in the Ural Mountains of Russia. Perhaps as many as 90 percent of all species then alive vanished. Another mass extinction took place late in the Triassic Period, some 202 million years ago, from the Latin word *trias*, meaning three. About 50 percent of all species perished. Researchers into the late Triassic extinction have come up with conflicting evidence about its cause. Some report finding high levels of iridium in late Triassic sediments in Austria while others report finding shocked quartz at the same level in Italy. Still others point to the huge Manicouagan impact crater in eastern Canada as the "smoking asteroid-gun." More evidence is needed before an asteroid or comet strike can be linked to the Triassic extinctions.

All of the cosmic missiles mentioned so far are dwarfed by one that plunged into Earth about four billion years ago, according to NASA scientist Luke Dones and Scott Tremaine, director of the Canadian Institute for Theoretical Astrophysics. The two envision a Mars-size object (6,800 kilometers across) smashing into Earth with a force that accounts for our planet's rapid rotation. At the same time, they suggest, matter that

splashed off became the Moon. Dones has said that Mercury, Venus, and Mars also may have acquired their rotational speeds from large impacts.

That we have been hit numerous times in the past cannot be doubted, and that we surely will be hit again is equally certain. The two questions are: When? And is there anything we can do to avoid an impending collision?

This Mariner *photograph of Mercury shows an untold number of craters caused by cosmic debris smashing into the planet early in the life of the Solar System. The Moon, Mars, and moons of the giant planets also have numerous craters, testifying to the countless impacts by asteroids, comets, and other space debris over the past hundreds of millions of years.*   NASA PHOTO

NEED *for an* EARLY WARNING SYSTEM

66 "*T*here is a 1 in 10,000 chance that a large (about 2-kilo-meter) asteroid or comet will collide with Earth during the next century, disrupting the ecosphere and killing a large fraction of the world's population," according to two scientists writing in the 6 January 1994 issue of the British science magazine *Nature*.

In 1990 the American Institute of Aeronautics and Astronautics warned that studies should be made of the asteroid threat to the global environment, and of means to prevent asteroid or comet impacts. The U.S. House of Representatives responded by ordering NASA to take up the matter. NASA organized the two workshops mentioned earlier. One was told to examine our present ability to detect and track asteroids and comets, and then to recommend ways of improving our detection capabilities. The other was to recommend ways of destroying or otherwise evading collisions with life-threatening NEOs.

FIRST DETECTION, THEN EVASION OR DESTRUCTION

The first workshop reported that our present state of knowledge of NEOs is not very good. "Of the estimated 2,000 NEOs with diameters of one kilometer or more, the precise orbits of less than 100 are known," according to the workshop report. The report went on to say that if we detected a large NEO on a collision course with Earth "we are presently quite unprepared to deal with it in an organized manner."

However, workshop members agreed that a network of telescopes dedicated to the detection of NEOs could be put in place over the next ten years. Such an asteroid-watch system would be able to detect "perhaps 90 percent of the short-period asteroids whose size could constitute a major threat to all of humanity," according to the report. Although it would take ten years to put such a global early warning system in place, the report points out that we presently have the rocket and explosives technologies "capable of eliminating [an asteroid or comet] threat, provided that we institute the appropriate research and development efforts.... The guidance, tracking, and homing technologies developed by the Department of Defense and the nuclear explosives technologies developed by the Department of Energy are directly applicable to the deflection or destruction of these objects."

The threat from a 1 kilometer-size NEO to your hometown during your lifetime is low, according to statistics. Comet discoverer Shoemaker has said there is a 12 to 40 percent chance of another Tunguska impact in the next seventy-five years. What such numbers don't tell us is that the fireball could come seventy-five years from now, or this year, or somewhere in between, or not at all. If you are a pessimist, you can say that so far we have been lucky. If you are an optimist, you can say that 1908 happened to be a bad year, but not as bad as 66 million years ago. In either case, should luck fail the results could be horrendous. Imagine an early warning system bulletin announcing that New York City is to be targeted at 9:45 A.M. by a 1-kilometer asteroid three days from the time of the announcement. Now imagine trying to evacuate in three days the greater New York City area with its more than 7 million people, or to evacuate Chicago, Los Angeles, Miami, Tokyo, London, or any other major city.

Our ability to protect the planet from a NEO on a collision course with us depends on four things—the object's size, its speed, the amount of warning time, and our technological ability to deal with the object, either to destroy it or to interfere with its flight path to alter its course.

The larger and faster the object and the shorter the warning time, the more difficult it would be to take evasive action. As Academician Vasiliev reminds us in the Preface, it also is important to know about the composition of cosmic invaders if we are to deal with them. And that is why continued investigation into the composition of the Apollo Objects, and the Tunguska object, is important to the well being of people of all nations.

Although we generally know something about the composition of asteroids and comets, we do not know the composition of very many specific asteroids or specific comets. In general, there are three large classes of objects. Most of the asteroids are rocky while others are metal. The metal ones are more massive and tend to survive their journey through the atmosphere and strike the surface of Earth. The stony ones tend to burn up as they streak down into dense layers of the air, at least the smaller ones do. Comets seem to be ice balls containing frozen water and other ices, rocky and metallic material of unknown particle size, and organic compounds; however, there is no *detailed* knowledge of the composition of comets, and there will not be until we intercept one with a space probe and dig into its nucleus.

NUCLEAR WARHEADS FOR THE COSMOS

What are some of the schemes that workshop members came up with for dealing with an Earth-threatening NEO? It now seems that the nuclear weapons technology that for so long has gripped the world in fear is the only technology that may be able to ward off disaster from errant asteroids and comets. The idea would be to mount a nuclear warhead atop a rocket and send the rocket on a course that would intercept the NEO and blow it to bits safely away from Earth. Such a nuclear explosive might be implanted within the nucleus of a large comet or beneath the surface of a "soft" rocky object and then detonated to pulverize the object. To do this, workshop members foresee a vehicle with an engine for maneuvering and landing on the object. It would also need a device to bore beneath the surface. Although this scheme could destroy the asteroid or comet, there is also the possibility of shattering the object into a shotgunlike blast that might end up hitting Earth as a destructive swarm of cosmic missiles instead of an equally destructive single bullet.

Nuclear devices exploded near or at the surface of a metallic or especially large stony asteroid could nudge the object into an orbit that would detour around Earth. Another possibility considered by workshop members was flying a manned mission to the intruder, landing on it, and then fitting it with thrusters that would propel the object away from Earth. To avoid flying a rocket out to meet a NEO, laser guns operated from Earth, or from the Moon, might be used to nudge the intruder off course. One advantage of the laser approach would be that we could observe the effects of each burst on the object's orbit and adjust successive bursts accordingly. The approach most favored by workshop members was exploding a nuclear warhead at an appropriate distance from the NEO to alter its course so that it misses hitting Earth.

"BRILLIANT MOUNTAINS"

One of the most imaginative proposals made at the workshop was given the name "Brilliant Mountains." Nuclear rockets would be sent out to capture small nearby asteroids and then return with them and shepherd them into orbit around Earth where the flock would be kept in storage. Asteroids with masses of 1,000 to 10,000 tons could be parked in Earth orbit. Then in the event an incoming NEO was found to be on a collision course with us, a Brilliant Mountain of just the right mass could be nudged out of Earth's orbit and into a new orbit that would intercept the NEO and destroy it at a safe distance from Earth. Hopefully, the resulting shotgun fragments would miss Earth.

The workshop concluded with this thought: "Presently there is no organized program to address the NEO hazard. A decision to proceed should not be delayed in anticipation that new data will soon substantially modify our present understanding. The estimated level of threat merits a near-term response. We should begin now."

In a tentative way we have. In January 1994 NASA said it was planning to send a spacecraft to NEO 433 Eros, a killer asteroid about 35 kilometers in diameter. The robot craft is planned for launch early in 1996. If all goes well, by late summer it will be among the main-belt asteroids beyond Mars. It will then swing back on a course toward Earth and in early 1998 be given a gravity boost that will take it to 433 Eros in December. For a year the craft will orbit the asteroid from a distance as close as 24 kilometers, close enough to see features as small as a meter across. If successful, the NEAR mission (Near Earth Asteroid Rendezvous) will give us our first close-up view of a NEO.

One of the main ideas in this book, and one emphasized in the NASA workshops, is that an early warning system to detect cosmic invaders, and a means to destroy them before they destroy us, is the concern of every nation. It is, therefore, an effort that requires global cooperation. The task will not be easy because it calls for political as well as financial cooperation. For example, one requirement would be the development of a very powerful (100-megaton) nuclear explosive, one about five times the force of the asteroid impact that blasted out Arizona's Meteor Crater. Its development would further require several test explosions. But under existing and projected nuclear test-ban treaties, such a program could not be started.

If the world waits for a cosmic visitor known to be on a collision course with Earth before approving an international cooperative interception program, it might be too late. Both Russia and the United States still have numerous nuclear explosives left over from the cold war. One thing both nations could do, before destroying their stockpiles, is to agree on which ones might be useful for defense against disaster-threatening near-Earth objects. Then the explosives could be put aside under international safeguard until more effective defense techniques could be designed and put "on-line."

In addition to NASA's study of NEOs, the International Astronomical Union also is studying the problem of asteroid hazards. In October of 1991 the former Soviet Union held an all-Union conference on the subject. Cosmic impacts unquestionably are everybody's concern.

Clearly, we must continue to study the Tunguska event in order to identify the object that "split the sky apart." In some small but significant way a knowledge of what the object was just might help prepare us for the next local impact that could demolish Chicago, Paris, London, or Tokyo. And equally clearly, we must realize that the next Tunguska may occur not on a local but on a global scale and blast humanity back into the Stone Age. Whether the next catastrophe will be on a local or global scale, we do not know. It is not though, a matter of *if* one or the other will happen, but *when*.

The ultimate question is "Will we be ready?"

FURTHER READING

Angier, Natalie. "Did Comets Kill the Dinosaurs?" *Time* (6 May 1985), pp. 70–83.

Baxter, John, and Thomas Atkins. *The Fire Came By: The Riddle of the Great Siberian Explosion.* Garden City, N.Y.: Doubleday & Company, Inc., 1976.

Beatty, J. Kelly. "Impacts Revealed." *Sky & Telescope* (February 1994), pp. 26–27.

Begley, Sharon. "The Science of Doom." *Newsweek* (23 November 1992), pp. 56–63.

Ben-Menahem, Ari. "Source Parameters of the Siberian Explosion of June 30, 1908, from Analysis and Synthesis of Seismic Signals at Four Stations." *Physics of the Earth and Planetary Interiors*, Vol. 11 (1975), pp. 1–35.

Benton, Michael J. "Late Triassic Extinctions and the Origin of the Dinosaurs." *Science*, Vol. 260 (7 May 1993), pp. 769–770.

Boyarkina, A. P., V. A. Bronshten, and A. K. Stanyukovich. "Non-stationary interactions of the shock waves in the gas-dynamical problems of the meteorites." In *Interactions of the Meteoric Matter with the Earth* (in Russian). Novosibirsk:

Nauka (Siberian Branch), pp. 138–156.

Brown, John C., and David W. Hughes. "Tunguska's comet and non-thermal ^{14}C production in the atmosphere." *Nature*, Vol. 268 (11 August 1977), pp. 512–514.

Chaikin, Andrew. "Target: Tunguska." *Sky & Telescope* (January 1984), pp. 18–21.

Chapman, Clark R., and David Morrison. "Impacts on the Earth by asteroids and comets: assessing the hazard." *Nature*, Vol. 367 (6 January 1994), pp. 33–39.

Chyba, Christopher. "Death From the Sky." *Astronomy* (December 1993), pp. 38–45.

Chyba, Christopher, Paul J. Thomas, and Kevin J. Zahnie. "The 1908 Tunguska explosion: atmospheric disruption of a stony asteroid." *Nature*, Vol. 361 (7 January 1993), pp. 40–44.

Cowan, C., C. R. Atluri, and W. F. Libby. "Possible Anti-Matter Content of the Tunguska Meteor of 1908." *Nature*, Vol. 206, no. 4987 (1965), pp. 861–865.

Cowen, Ron. "Rocky Relics." *Science News* (5 February 1994), pp. 88–90.

D'Alessio, S. J. D., and A. A. Harms. "The Nuclear and Aerial Dynamics of the Tunguska Event." *Planetary and Space Science*, Vol. 37 (1989), pp. 329–340.

Dmitriev, A. N., and V. K. Zhuravlev. "The Tunguska Phenomenon of 1908—a Coronal Microtransient." *Geologiya i Geofizika*, Vol. 27, no. 4 (1986), pp. 10–19.

Folger, Tim. "This Battered Earth." *Discover* (January 1994), pp. 32–34.

Gaffey, Michael J. "Forging an Asteroid-Meteorite Link." *Science*, Vol. 260 (9 April 1993), pp. 167–168.

Gallant, Roy A. "The Sky Has Split Apart." *Sky & Telescope* (June 1994), cover and pp. 38–43.

———. "Tunguska Revisted." *Meteorite!* (February 1995), cover and pp. 8–11.

Gehrels, Tom, ed. *Hazards Due to Comets and Asteroids.* University of Arizona Press, 1994.

Glass, Billy P. "Silicate Spherules from Tunguska Impact Area: Electron Microprobe Analysis." *Science,* Vol. 164 (2 May 1969), pp. 547–549.

Jackson, A. A., and Michael P. Ryan. "Was the Tungus Event due to a Black Hole?" *Nature,* Vol. 245 (14 September 1973), pp. 88–89.

Kerr, Richard A. "Huge Impact Is Favored K-T Boundary Killer." *Science,* Vol. 242 (11 November 1988), pp. 865–867.

———. "A Source Found for Earth's Commonest Meteorites." *Science,* Vol. 261 (23 July 1993), p. 427.

Kirova, O. A. "Scattered Matter from the Area of Fall of the Tunguska Cometary Meteorite." Annals New York Academy of Sciences (1964), pp. 235-242.

Kolesnikov, E. M. "Search for traces of Tunguska cosmic body dispersed matter." *Meteoritics,* Vol. 24, no. 4 (1989), p. 288.

Korobeinikov, V. P., S. B. Gusev, P. I. Chushkin, and L. V. Shurshalov. "Mathematical model and computation of the Tunguska meteorite explosion." *Acta Astronautica,* Vol. 3 (1976), pp. 615–622.

Krinov, E. L. *Giant Meteorites.* New York: Pergamon Press, 1966.

———. *Principles of Meteoritics.* New York: Pergamon Press, 1960.

Kulik, L. A. "The Problem of the Impact Area of the Tunguska Meteorite of 1908." *Doklady Akad.* Nauk SSSR *(A),* no. 23 (1927), pp. 399–402.

La Paz, Lincoln. "Meteorite Craters and the Hypothesis of the Existence of Contraterrene Meteorites." *Contributions of the Society for Research on Meteorites,* Vol. 2, no. 4 (1941), pp. 244–247.

Levin, B. Yu., and V. A. Bronshten. "The Tunguska Event and the Meteors with Terminal Flares." *Meteoritics,* Vol. 21, no. 2 (30 June 1986), pp. 199–215.

Matthews, Robert. "A Rocky Watch for Earthbound Asteroids." *Science*, Vol. 255 (6 March 1992), pp. 1204–1205.

Melosh, H. J. "Tunguska comes down to Earth." *Nature*, Vol. 361 (7 January 1993), pp. 14–15.

———. and I. V. Nemchinov. "Solar asteroid diversion." *Nature*, Vol. 366 (4 November 1993), pp. 21–22.

Monastersky, R. "Cretaceous die-offs: A tale of two comets?" *Science News*, Vol. 143 (3 April 1993), pp. 212–213.

———. "Cretaceous extinctions: The strikes add up." *Science News* Vol. 143 (19 June 1993), p. 391.

———. "Impact Wars." *Science News*, Vol. 145 (5 March 1994), pp. 156–157.

Mowat, Farley. *The Siberians*. Boston: Little, Brown and Company, 1970.

National Aeronautics and Space Administration (NASA). *Near-Earth-Object Interception Workshop* (August 31, 1992).

Ostro, S. J., *et al.* "Asteroid 1986 DA: Radar Evidence for a Metallic Composition." *Science*, Vol. 252 (7 June 1991), pp. 1399–1404.

Rasmussen, K. L., H. B. Clausen, and T. Risbo. "Nitrate in the Greenland Ice Sheet in the Years Following the 1908 Tunguska Event." *Icarus*, Vol. 58 (1984), pp. 101–108.

Schroder, W. "An Additional Note on the So-Called Tunguska Event." *Planetary and Space Science*, Vol. 38, no. 10 (1990), pp. 1351–53.

Sekanina, Z. "The Tunguska Event: No Cometary Signature in Evidence." *The Astronomical Journal*, Vol. 88, no. 9 (September 1983), pp. 1382–1413.

Suslov, I. M. "In Search of the Great Meteorite of 1908." *Mirovedenie*, Vol. 16, no. 1 (1927), pp. 13–18.

Trayner, Chris. "Perplexities of the Tunguska Meteorite." *The Observatory*, Vol. 114, no. 1122 (October 1994), pp. 227–231.

Vasiliev. N. V. "On some anomalous effects related to the

Tunguska meteorite fall." In *Cosmic Materials on the Earth* [in Russian]. Novosibirsk: Nauka (1976).

———. "The problem of the Tunguska meteorite." *Zemlya 1 Vselennaya*, no. 1 (1975).

Waldrop, M. Mitchell. "After the Fall." *Science*, Vol. 238 (26 February 1988), p. 977.

Wetherill, George W. "Apollo Objects." *Scientific American*, Vol. 240, no. 3 (March 1979), pp. 54–65.

"When Worlds Don't Collide: Earth Escapes." *Science*, Vol. 261 (9 July 1993), p. 159.

Zbik, Marek. "Morphology of the Outermost Shells of the Tunguska Black Magnetic Spherules." *Journal of Geophysical Research*, Vol. 89, Supplement, (15 February 1984), pp. B605–B611.

Zotkin, I. T., and M. A. Tsikulin. "Simulation of the Explosion of the Tungus Meteorite." *Soviet Physics—Doklady*, Vol. 11, no. 3 (September 1966), pp. 183–186.

"Minor Planet Observer" (for use with Windows) is the title of a computer software program for finding the positions of more than 5,400 asteroids, according to the software supplier, Andromeda Software, Inc., P.O. Box 605, Amherst, NY 14226.

INDEX

Acid rains, 138
Aerial survey, 45, 89, 94, 96, 97-98
Ahnighito meteorite, 35
Aksenov, Ivan, 11, 29
Aksenov, Pavel, 14, 54, 57
Akulina, 14, 15
Altov, T., 122
Alvarez, Luis and Walter, 135-136
American Institute of Aeronautics and Astronautics, 142
Amors, 133
Amur River Basin, 8
Anavar. *See* Vanavara
Anderson, Carl D., 119
Angara River, 28, 50, 61, 63
Animism, 4
Ankov, S., 13
Antimatter hypothesis, 110, 118-120
Anton Chekhov (ship), 23
Apollo objects, 132-133, 144
Argon 39, 110, 112
Arizona Meteor Crater, 42-43, 48, 147
Around the World (Vokrug Sveta), 101
Astapovich, I. S., 107
Asteroids
  composition of, 132, 144
  current scientific knowledge on,

131-134
  discovery of, 129-130
  early warning system for, 142-147
  Earth-impacts by, xiv, 135-141
  meteorites from, 32, 35
  near-Earth approaches of, 126-129
  species extinctions caused by, 135-136
  Tunguska explosion and, 116-118
Astronomical Journal, 117, 118
Atens, 133
Atluri, C. R., 119
Atmospheric pressure changes, 6
Atomic bomb, xiv, 100-101

Baikal, Lake, 101
Banya, 59, 85
Base Camp, 85-90, 92, 94, 96, 98
Biot, Jean B., 32
Bird studies, 94-95
Black hole hypothesis, 120-122
Black rain, 4
Bode, Johann, 129
Bolides, 41, 106
Bottger, Tatiana, 114
Boyarkina, Alyona, 114, 115-116

Brilliant Mountains proposal, 146
Bryukhanova, Marfa, 14

Cambrian period, 139
Cape York, Greenland, 35
Carbon 14, 119
Cascade, Mount, 72, 76
Chamba River, 11, 13, 14, 15, 54, 58, 64, 73, 83, 84
Chekhov, Anton, 21, 22-23
Chicxulub Crater, 137, 138
Churgim Creek, 11, 72, 73, 74, 85, 98
Churgim Heights, 76
Chuvar Range, 13
Chyba, C. F., 116-118, 126
Colorado Museum of Natural History, 82
Comets
  composition of, 107, 109, 144
  described, 107-109
  early warning system for, 142-147
  meteor showers and, 33
  Tunguska explosion and, 107, 110-115, 117-118
Committee on Meteorites and Cosmic Dust, 105
Cowan, Clyde, 119

153

Craters
  from meteorites, 125,
    126, 127, 137
  on other planets,
    140-141
  Suslov crater, 89-94,
    104
  at Tunguska site, 79,
    80, 83, 89
  worldwide map of, 125
Cretaceous Period,
  134-136, 138-139

Daunov, Pavel, 14
Deep Bay Crater, 126
Dickson, 23
Dinosaurs, 134-135
"The Dock," 59, 67, 68,
  70, 71, 76, 85, 89,
  90
Dones, Luke, 139
Doonov, Petr and Vasiliy,
  13
Drilling explorations,
  92-94
Dronov, S., 11
Dzhenkhoul, Ivan, 14
Dzhenkoul, Vasiliy, 11,
  72, 73

Earthquake disasters,
  18-19
Ekaterinburg, 22
Eldredge, Niles, 138-139
Evenki. *See* Tungus peo-
  ple
Expedition Research
  Commission, 48
Expeditions, Tunguska
  by Florensky, 103-104
  by Kulik, 26, 48-60,
    72-81, 83-88, 89-99
  Interdisciplinary
    Independent
    Expedition (IIE),
    105-106, 115
  International Tunguska
    Expedition, 102
Extinctions, earthwide,
  135-136, 138-139

Falling stars, 32
Federov, Nickolai, 2
Fegley, Bruce, 138
Fesenkov, V., 104, 105,
  110
"Filimonovo meteorite," 44
Flight path, 47-48
Florensky, Kirill, 103-106
Florensky, P., 103

Food storage huts, 85
Forests
  new plant growth in,
    xvi, 104-105
  stripped, 76, 77, 78-79
Fossil discoveries, 70,
  71
French Academy of
  Sciences, 31

Gehrels, Tom, 128
Geologic periods, 134
Glass, Billy P., 112
Goblins, 121
Goda, M. Patrick, 118
Goddard Space Flight
  Center, 112
Gorbachev, Mikhail, 102
Great Cauldron, 77
"Guest from the Cosmos,
  A" (Kazantsev), 102
Gyulikh, 48

Hawking, Stephen, 121
Hayden Planetarium, 33
Helin, Eleanor, 128
Hills, Jack G., 118
Hiroshima, Japan, xiv,
  100-101
Hoba West meteorite,
  34-35

Ikeya-Seki comet, 108
Ilich, Vasiliy, 17
*In Search of the Tunguska
  Wonder* (Kulik), 76, 79
Interdisciplinary
  Independent
  Expedition (IIE),
  105-106, 115
International
  Astronomical Union,
  147
International Tunguska
  Expedition, 102
Iridium, 136-137, 139
Irkutsk, 44
Irkutsk Magnetic and
  Meteorological
  Observatory, 47
Iron meteorites, 32, 88,
  103
Isotope concentrations,
  113-115
Ivanova, Lydia, 30

Jablonksi, David, 137
Jackson, A. A., 121
Jefferson, Thomas, 31
Junghans, Karin, 116

Kama River, 22
Kandyba, Yuriy, 13n, 29,
  30, 58, 60-61, 72, 75,
  87, 94-96
Kansk, 40-41, 44
Kara Sea, 23
Kazantsev, Aleksander,
  100-102, 119
Kezhemskoye, 37-38
Kezhma, 50-51, 61, 83,
  87, 93, 96
"Khatanga meteorite," 48
Khavarkikta River, 11, 13
Khushmo River, 13, 14,
  15, 57, 58-59, 67,
  69-71, 85
Kimchu River, 11, 13
Kolesnikov, Evgeniy,
  110-115, 119
Kolkhoz, 63
Korobeinikov, V. P., 118
Kosolapov, M., 14
Krakatoa, 18
Krasnoyarian, 37
Krasnoyarsk, 23, 25
Krinov, E. L., 31, 43, 78,
  89, 93-94, 104, 107,
  113
K/T boundary layer,
  136-137
Kuiper, G. P., 107
Kuiper belt, 107
Kulik, Leonid Alexeivich
  biographical sketch of,
    27, 30-32
  bird studies of, 94-95
  death of, 99
  epicenter expedition,
    72-81
  eyewitness interviews
    by, 10, 15-17, 44
  first expedition, 48-60
  last expeditions, 97-99
  learns of 1908 blast,
    36-41
  map of devastated area
    by, 56
  1928 expedition of,
    83-88
  1929-1930 expedition
    of 89-97
  political deception by,
    87-88
  surveys by, 85, 86,
    87-89

L'Aigle, France, 31-32
Lake Cheko, 11
Land surveys, 85, 89
La Paz, Lincoln, 119

Laser guns, 145
Lenin, Nikolai, 20
Libby, Willard, 119
Light nights, xv–xvi, 5-6, 19, 39-40, 117
London *Times*, 6
Lower Dulyushma River, 14-15
Lyuchetkan, 8-10, 15, 16-17, 46, 51-61, 76, 93

Machakugyr, 13
Magnetic disturbances, xvi, 6, 115
Magnetic surveys, 45, 85, 88, 98, 115
Magnetite, 103, 106
Magnetometers, 49, 88
Makirta River, 54
Manicouagan crater, 139
Maps
  of craters worldwide, 125
  of Siberian region, xvii–xviii
  of Tunguska explosion, 12, 56
Mareensk, 25
Martian hypothesis, 101, 119
Martian meteorite, 34
Melosh, H. J., 117
Mercury (planet), 140-141
Meteor Crater, Arizona, 42-43, 48
Meteorite!, 34
Meteorites
  composition of, 32
  craters formed by, xiv, 125, 126, 127, 137
  early warning system for, 142-147
  earth collisions of, 126-128
  history of, 34-35
  origins of, 31-33
Meteoritics, 34
Meteoroids, 32
Meteorological changes, 6
Meteors, 32
Meteor showers, 33-34
Micrometeorites, 32
Microspherules, 106-107, 112, 137
Mineralogical Museum of the Academy of Sciences, 30, 43
Mining, of Arizona

Meteor Crater, 42-43
Moscow People's Militia, 99
Moscow University, 110
Mosquitoes, Siberian, 25
Mowat, Farley, 21
Mul'tanovsky, 83

Nagorny, V. F., 39
NASA (National Aeronautics and Space Administra-tion), 124, 133, 142, 146-147
Nature, 121, 142
NEAR (Near Earth Asteroid Rendezvous) mission, 146
"Near-Earth-Object Interception Workshop," 129, 142
Near-Earth-Object Search Committee, 133
NEAs (Near-Earth Asteroids), 132
NEOs (Near-Earth Objects)
  classification of, 132-133
  destroying/deflecting, 145-147
  early warning system for, 142-144, 146-147
  renewed interest in, 124-129
Newspaper accounts of Tunguska explosion, 37-41
New York Times, 5-6
Night light displays. *See* Light nights
Night-shining clouds, xvi
Nizhne-Karelinsk, 40
Northern lights, 39
Novosibirsk, 24, 25
Nuclear devices, 145
Nuclear explosion theory, 101-103, 105

Obruchev, S. V., 46
October Revolution, 31
Ogdy (god of fire), 4, 27, 29, 48, 52, 53, 61, 64
Okhechen. *See* Aksenov, Pavel
Onkoul, Stepan Ilich, 15
Oort, Jan H., 107

Oort cloud, 107, 108

Peat samples, 110-115
Permafrost, 21, 89
Permian Period, 139
Piazzi, Giuseppi, 129
Plant growth, xvi, 104-105
Plasma hypothesis, 116
Plekhanov, G .F., 105
Podkamennaya Tunguska River. *See* Stony Tunguska River
Pokruta, 63
Potapovich, Ilya. *See* Lyuchetkan
Prinn, Ronald G., 138
"Problem of the Impact Area of the Tunguska Meteorite of 1908, The" (Kulik), 15
Puchki plant, 80

Rabinowitz, David I., 133
Radioactivity testing, 105
Reindeer, 10, 17, 63, 105
Remote sensing studies, 116
Rossovskaya, Kathy, 60, 68, 72, 102
Russian Academy of Sciences, 6, 15, 43, 98-99, 103
Ryan, Michael P., 121

Saint Petersburg, xiv
Sakura, 102
Sand Dune Hill, 75
Seismic waves, xvi
Sekanina, Zdenek, 117
Semenov, S., 14, 16, 47, 53
Semyonov, Yuri, 25
Shakharma, Mount, 55, 58, 76
Shamanism, 4, 27, 65-66, 74
Shaman Vasiliy, 73-74, 80
Shanyagir, 13
Shapley, Harlow, 107
Shoemaker, Eugene M., 134
Shoemaker-Levy 9, Comet, 133
Shooting stars, 32
Siberian region
  described, 22-25
  map, xviii–xix
  remoteness of, 19-22

taiga and tundra of,
25-26
Sikhote-Alin meteorite,
17, 103, 104
Silicate, 106, 112
Sobolev, 46
Soil profiles, 89
Soil samples, 103-106,
110-115
Southern Swamp, 72, 73,
76-77, 79, 83, 85, 89,
94, 96, 98, 104
Soviet Academy of
Sciences. *See* Russian
Academy of Sciences
"Spaceguard Survey, The,"
129, 142-143
Spas-Demensk, 99
Sphagnum plant samples,
110-112
Stalin, Joseph, 20
Stanly, S. M., 138
Sterlytomack, xiv
Stoikovich, Mount, 85
Stony meteorites, 32
Stony Tunguska River, xv,
3, 16, 44, 46, 51, 54,
63, 84, 97
Strukov, N., 69, 83, 84, 86
Superstitions, Tungus, 27,
29-30, 46, 52, 75
Susdalev, 28-30
Suslov, Innokenty, 9, 10, 15,
47, 49, 51, 75, 77, 88
Suslov crater, 90-94, 96,
112-113
Sytin, 83-84, 86-87

Tarkichonok, P., 13
Tayshet, 48
Telegraph-pole forest
in Hiroshima, Japan,
101
in Tunguska region, 76,
77, 78-79
Tepees, Tungus, 8-10
Tertiary Period, 135-136
Thomas, P. J., 116
Tomsk, 36, 44, 105
Tomsk Diocesan News, 39
Tomsk Technological
Institute, 100
Tomsk University, 31,
114, 115
Topographical survey, 85,
89

*Trading-Industrial Gazette
SPB, The*, 40
Trans-Siberian Railroad,
3-4, 20, 21, 24-26, 48,
83
Tree growth, xvi,
104-105
Tremaine, Scott, 139
Treptow Observatory, 5
Triassic Period, 139
Trotsky, Leon, 20
Tsvetkov, Valentin, 118
Tunguska explosion
antimatter hypothesis,
110, 118-120
asteroid hypothesis,
116-118
black hole hypothesis,
120-122
comet hypothesis, 107,
110-115, 117-118
current scientific
conclusions on,
xv–xvi, 123
described, 1-4
devastation caused by,
55-57
eyewitness accounts
on, 11-17, 44
flight path of object in,
47-48
human death toll of,
18-19
maps of, 12, 56
meteorite hypothesis,
91-94, 96-99, 104,
106-107
newspaper accounts of,
37-41
nuclear explosion
hypothesis, 101-103,
105, 110
plasma hypothesis, 116
tree growth following,
xvi, 104-105
Tunguska Marvel
(Zhuravlev & Zegel),
53
Tunguska region
Florensky's expedition
to, 103-104
Interdisciplinary
Independent
Expedition (IIE) to,
105-106, 115
International Tunguska

Expedition to, 102
Kulik's expeditions to,
26, 48-60, 72-81,
83-88, 89-99
preservation of, xvii
Tungus people
decline of, 63-65
eyewitness accounts
by, 11-17, 44
history of, 8, 61-65
respect for Kulik by,
72-74
shamanism and, 27,
65-66
superstitions of, 27,
29-30, 46, 52, 75-76
tepees of, 8-10

Ukagitkon River, 11
Ungava-Quebec Crater,
127
Upper Devonian Period,
139
Upper Lakura River, 13
Ural Mountains, 30

Vanavara, 14, 16, 20, 28,
46, 50, 51, 63-65, 80,
87, 92, 93, 97
Vasiliev, Academician
Nickolai, xiii–xvii, 5,
19, 85, 102, 122, 144
Vernadsky, Vladamir, 30,
43, 48, 83
Voronov, Vitaliy, 60-66,
67-72
Voznesensky, V., 47-48
Vronsky, B., 106

Whipple, Fred L., 107
White nights. *See* Light
nights
Williamette meteorite, 33

Yakochen, P., 14
Yavnel, A. A., 103, 104
Yenisei River, 8, 23
Yerineev, Ivan, 14
Yucatan Peninsula, 137,
138

Zahnele, K. J., 116
Zegel, F. U., 53
Zhuravlev, V. K., 53, 122
Zinsmeister, William, 139
Zolotov, A. V., 119